Primary Language Arts

Grade 6

NSC Edition

Josh Lury
Heather Raymond
Mitzie-Ann Jackson

The Publishers would like to thank the following for permission to reproduce copyright material.

Text credits

p.23: © Jamaica National Heritage Trust; p.36: © "THIS DAY IN 1962, "The Gleaner Company (Media) Limited; p.45: © Hodder and Stoughton Limited, First Aid Reader E: Crossing the Line and other stories; p.49: © James Berry, "Hot Earth, Cold Earth", Bloodaxe Books, 1995; p.52: © Hodder and Stoughton Limited, First Aid Reader D: A Narrow Escape and other stories; p.57: © Jamaica National Heritage Trust; p.76: © Rain by Valerie Bloom; p.221: Over the Roofs of the World (Insomniac Press, 2005), © Olive Senior; p.228: From Controlling the Silver. Copyright 2005 by Lorna Goodison. Used with permission of the University of Illinois Press; p.231: © Dis 'N Dat, Jamaica National Heritage Trust.

Photo credits

t = top, b = below, l = left, r = right, c = centre, b/g = background

p.10: (r) © PA Images/PA/Alamy.com, (l) © Keystone Press/KEYSTONE Pictures USA/Alamy; p.14: © Argus/stock.adobe.com; p.22: © africa/stock.adobe.com; p.23: (t) © Janusz Pienkowski/Shutterstock.com; (c) © vkilikov/stock.adobe.com; p.29: (tl) © PA Images/John Giles/Alamy.com, (tr) © David Levenson/Alamy.com; (cl) © PA Images/Yui Mok/Alamy.com, (cr) © Nina Reistad/Alamy.com; p.42: (t,c) © North Wind Picture Archives/Alamy.com, (bl) © Panoramic Images/Alamy.com, (br) © nicolebleck/stock.adobe.com; p.49: © happystock/stock.adobe.com; p.52: © Greg Johnston/Danita Delimont/Alamy.com; p.67: (tl) © PhotoSpirit/stock.adobe.com, (tr) © Greg Meland/stock.adobe.com, (bl) © mmuenzl/stock.adobe.com, (bc) © Konstantin Kulikov/stock.adobe.com, (br) © Joel/stock.adobe.com; p.76: © กรบูรษ วรดี/stock.adobe.com; p.81: © Siphosethu Fanti/peopleimages.com/stock.adobe.com; p.82: (tl) © Veniamin/stock.adobe.com, (cl) © Christophe Fouquin/stock.adobe.com, (r) © Vastram/stock.adobe.com; p.84: (tl) © Felix Mizioznikov/stock.adobe.com, (tr) © de Art/stock.adobe.com, (c) © Riccardo Niels Mayer/stock.adobe.com; p.102: (l) © DC Studio/stock.adobe.com, (r) © deagreez/stock.adobe.com; p.105: © sushi7688/stock.adobe.com; p.113: (tl) © Rawpixel.com/stock.adobe.com, (cl) © revers_jr/stock.adobe.com, (cr) © Inga Av/stock.adobe.com, (tr) © Prostock-studio/stock.adobe.com, (bl) © rakop_ton/stock.adobe.com, (br) © razihusin/stock.adobe.com; p.119: © Libor/stock.adobe.com, © taitai6769/stock.adobe.com, © Atiketta Sangasaeng/stock.adobe.com, © lukszczepanski/stock.adobe.com, © fotobieshutterb/stock.adobe.com, © Suriyo/stock.adobe.com, © vkph/stock.adobe.com, © Retouch man/stock.adobe.com, © GraphicsRF/stock.adobe.com; p.127: (tl) © TimeLineArtist/Shutterstock.com, (tr) © Destina/stock.adobe.com, (br) © Delphotostock/stock.adobe.com; p.132: © Martin/stock.adobe.com; p.136: © Micah C/peopleimages.com/stock.adobe.com; p.139: © Summit Art Creations/stock.adobe.com; p.143: © Mike Mareen/stock.adobe.com; p.171: (tl) © twinsterphoto/stock.adobe.com, (tr) © .shock/stock.adobe.com, (b) © Anatoliy Karlyuk/stock.adobe.com; p.177: (l) © Mongkolchon/stock.adobe.com, (c) © peopleimages.com/stock.adobe.com, (r) © dr322/stock.adobe.com; p.179: © Studio Romantic/stock.adobe.com; p.184: © Alila Medical Media/stock.adobe.com; p.188: © LuckySoul/stock.adobe.com; p.197: © Lumos sp/stock.adobe.com; p.200: © Volha Hlinskaya/stock.adobe.com; p.203: (tl) © Mikael Damkier/stock.adobe.com, (tc) © paulaphoto/stock.adobe.com, (tr) © Olesia Bilkei/stock.adobe.com, (bl) © Ranta Images/stock.adobe.com, (bc) © Drobot Dean/stock.adobe.com, (br) © Ranta Images/stock.adobe.com; p.207: © Daniel Ernst/stock.adobe.com, © ajr_images/stock.adobe.com, © michael spring/stock.adobe.com; p.216: © Speedfighter/stock.adobe.com; p.229: © Annatamila/stock.adobe.com.

Although every effort has been made to ensure that website addresses are correct at time of going to press, Hodder Education cannot be held responsible for the content of any website mentioned in this book. It is sometimes possible to find a relocated web page by typing in the address of the home page for a website in the URL window of your browser.

Hachette UK's policy is to use papers that are natural, renewable and recyclable products and made from wood grown in well-managed forests and other controlled sources. The logging and manufacturing processes are expected to conform to the environmental regulations of the country of origin.

To order, please visit www.hoddereducation.com or contact Customer Service at education@hachette.co.uk / +44 (0)1235 827827.

ISBN: 9781398356306

© Josh Lury, Heather Raymond, Mitzie-Ann Jackson and Hodder & Stoughton Limited 2024

This edition published in 2024 by

Hodder Education,

An Hachette UK Company

Carmelite House

50 Victoria Embankment

London EC4Y 0DZ

www.hoddereducation.com

Impression number 10 9 8 7 6 5 4 3 2 1

Year 2027 2026 2025 2024

All rights reserved. Apart from any use permitted under UK copyright law, no part of this publication may be reproduced or transmitted in any form or by any means, electronic or mechanical, including photocopying and recording, or held within any information storage and retrieval system, without permission in writing from the publisher or under licence from the Copyright Licensing Agency Limited. Further details of such licences (for reprographic reproduction) may be obtained from the Copyright Licensing Agency Limited, www.cla.co.uk

Cover illustration by Heather Clarke c/o D'Avila Illustration Agency.

Illustrations by David Blaine, Magriet Brink, Leo Daly, Susan Abrahams, Ruth Frances and Hyphen S.A.

Typeset by Hyphen S.A.

Printed in Spain

A catalogue record for this title is available from the British Library.

Contents

Contents.. 3

Term 1 **Unit 1**
Culture and heritage

Project 1: An independent country............. 10

Speaking and listening: Discuss and analyse photographs; listen to a reading and make notes; identify key information in a verbal account 10

Word builder: Vocabulary about independence; definitions; pronunciation; silent letters; prefixes and suffixes........................ 12

Let's read: Identify text types; locate information using headings; identify key topic sentences; use of headings, introduction, bullet points, captions; summarise; identify intended audience; plan research work..................................... 14

Grammar builder: Concrete and abstract nouns 17

Let's write: Write formal letters 19

Project 2: Our cultural heritage 21

Speaking and listening: Research, prepare and conduct a class debate about Jamaican culture.. 21

Word builder: Vocabulary about Jamaican culture; spelling; use mind maps to categorise vocabulary 22

Let's read: Read and answer questions about Jamaican National Heroes; research further information by skimming, collecting references and using mind maps... 23

Grammar builder: Interrogative pronouns; ask questions in the past, present and future tenses 26

Let's write: Plan and write a script; review and express an opinion... 28

Project 3: Then and now................................. 29

Speaking and listening: Discuss chronological order by observing photographs; describe a scene in Jamaican Creole and Standard Jamaican English 29

Word builder: Vocabulary including homophones; correct false use of homophones... 30

Let's read: Identify relevant information; identify and categorise linking words; understand chronological order; compare and contrast two sets... 31

Grammar builder: Before/after comparison and linking words; sequencing words; additional and contrasting links 34

Let's write: Write a journal entry using a Venn diagram, linking words and phrases 35

Project 4: It was in the news........................... 36

Speaking and listening: Listen to a reading and make notes; discuss questions and predict answers.. 36

Word builder: Identify prefixes and root words; misused homophones; Jamaican Creole and Standard Jamaican English use 37

Let's read: Read a news report and answer questions; comment on a title; consider consequences 38

Grammar builder: Plan paragraphs; paragraph structure; write opening and concluding sentences 40

Let's write: Write a news report; plan main ideas, paragraphs; write details; check and edit... 41

Project 5: Stories from the past 42

Speaking and listening: Respond to pictures; factual and emotional thinking; share ideas..... 42

Word builder: Suffixes; adjectives; transform nouns and verbs into adjectives; use adjectives to change meanings..................... 44

Let's read: Compare and contrast fiction and non-fiction; identify purpose of a text; describe different writing techniques; rhetorical questions 45

Grammar builder: Main and subordinate clauses; conjunctions; sentence construction.... 47

Let's write: Plan and undertake a longer writing project; use a visual organiser; use visual stimuli; discuss story techniques: characters, openings, suspense, description; make a first draft 48

Project 6: Jamaican literature 49

Speaking and listening: Listen and respond to a poem; ask and answer questions; perform the poem 49

Word builder: Inferences from context; mnemonics 51

Let's read: Read an excerpt from a longer story; identify purpose of text; identify the main event; compare and contrast with other texts; identify writing techniques involving adjectives, dialogue, sound effects and questions 52

Grammar builder: Subordinate and relative clauses; relative pronouns; subject-verb agreement 54

Let's write: Continue work on the longer writing project; edit and improve; techniques for improving story openings 55

Term 1 Unit 1 Review and assessment 57

Term 1 Unit 2
The physical environment

Project 7: An island of contrasts 59

Speaking and listening: Focused listening, using listening techniques 59

Word builder: Write definitions; construct sentences; use spelling techniques 61

Let's read: Recognise the viewpoint and purpose of text; identify positive and negative viewpoints; use and read maps; techniques for understanding words' meanings 62

Grammar builder: Adjectives that show viewpoint 65

Let's write: Awareness of personal response to written stimuli; show viewpoint in writing 67

Project 8: Fact or opinion? 68

Speaking and listening: Listen for facts and opinions; understand and explain the difference between objective and subjective writing 68

Word builder: Root words and word families; construct sentences 70

Let's read: Identify facts and opinions; use question words to extract information from texts 71

Grammar builder: Concrete and abstract nouns; understand and explain noun types 73

Let's write: Write a presentation including technical vocabulary and facts; write a paragraph expressing viewpoint; give and receive feedback; use a listening focus chart 74

Project 9: Up in the mountains 76

Speaking and listening: Listen to a poem and answer questions; identify poetic features; personification 76

Word builder: Spelling rules in word families; suffixes; double consonants; homophones 78

Let's read: Read and respond to poetry; understand transformation and personification; assist comprehension by reading expressively 79

Grammar builder: Adjectives and adverbs; modify verbs with adverbs 81

Let's write: Personification in writing; figurative language and storyboarding; invoke the senses in writing; write with anticipation and feeling 82

Project 10: Pictures that tell stories 84

Speaking and listening: Proverbs and sayings in Jamaican Creole and Standard Jamaican English; picture cues; discuss information obtained from pictures; identify facts and opinions 84

Word builder: Homonyms, antonyms, synonyms; use nouns, adjectives and verbs to describe pictures 86

Let's read: Read and respond to texts; answer *true* or *false* questions; collect and interpret data; read graphs to extract information and make predictions 87

Grammar builder: Conjunctions; simple, compound and complex sentences 89

Contents

Let's write: Plan, prepare and create a presentation about a problem; write about cause and effect using visuals to enhance presentation and language appropriate to the task 91

Project 11: What if there is a tsunami? 93

Speaking and listening: Hypothetical questions; use question words: what, who, why, how, where, when; share response with class; ask follow-up questions 93

Word builder: Syllabification; use a dictionary 95

Let's read: Narrative of speculative texts; answer comprehension questions; summarise; think hypothetically 96

Grammar builder: Demonstrative pronouns and adjectives; singular and plural; possessive pronouns 97

Let's write: Use a storyboard to complete a story; sequencing phrases; understand the pattern and structure of a story; plan, write and redraft a story, using feedback from others 99

Project 12: The aftermath 102

Speaking and listening: Work in groups to plan, rehearse and act out a news report about a disaster 102

Word builder: Syllabification; use a dictionary; compile definitions for selected words; identify prefixes, suffixes and unusual spelling patterns; use different spelling strategies 104

Let's read: Choose a headline for a news report; summarise; understand and describe the viewpoint; inference; fact and opinion; subjectivity and objectivity; critical and analytical reading 105

Grammar builder: Abstract and concrete nouns; demonstrative pronouns; linking phrases and conjunctions; adjectives and adverbs; ask questions; main and subordinate clauses 107

Let's write: Write a persuasive text; personification; use an editor's checklist; use prompts or a paragraph planner 108

Term 1 Unit 2 Review and assessment 110

Term 2 Unit 1
Energy and matter, light and sound

Project 13: Light in our lives 112

Speaking and listening: Identify prior knowledge; discuss and agree rules for classroom communication; discuss responses to visual stimulus; differentiate facts and opinions 112

Word builder: Use a dictionary; identify spelling patterns; prefixes and suffixes; homonyms and homophones 114

Let's read: Skim to assess a text; identify fact and opinion; define words in context; skim and scan for specific information; prepare a reference list 116

Grammar builder: Verb tenses and modal auxiliaries 119

Let's write: Write in paragraphs; write a journal; use reference lists and visual organisers 121

Project 14: Light 122

Speaking and listening: Complete sentences from dictation; ask open questions; prepare a vox pop programme on a science subject; act out vox pop interviews; categorise answers 122

Word builder: Identify definitions of technical words; create a word grid; identify and define words with prefix 'photo'; create a glossary 124

Let's read: Make predictions; verify information; create diagrammatic forms of information based on written text 126

Grammar builder: Construct sentences using pronouns, verbs and modal auxiliaries; observe the effect of modal auxiliaries on main verbs 128

Let's write: A class game writing sentences in groups; write a scientific explanation using planned paragraphs 129

Project 15: Sounds in our lives 130

Speaking and listening: Research and present a report on given scientific topic; listen attentively and take notes 130

5

Word builder: Vocabulary about sounds; write definitions; create and solve anagrams 131

Let's read: Comprehension questions; distinguish fact from opinion; skim a text; express and justify an opinion; define phrase in context 132

Grammar builder: The past perfect tenses ... 134

Let's write: Summarise a text; write research summaries 136

Project 16: The science of sound 137

Speaking and listening: Play games using sound effects, miming and actions; prepare and deliver a presentation; ask and answer questions 137

Word builder: Suffixes; spelling patterns in root words; pronunciation; letter combinations with multiple sounds 138

Let's read: Read factual texts and answer questions; compare and contrast; summarise 139

Grammar builder: Demonstrative pronouns .. 141

Let's write: Write a detailed paragraph; writing a scientific, objective text 142

Project 17: Sounds of science 143

Speaking and listening: Listen to and repeat poetry; echoing: rhythm, volume and intonation 143

Word builder: Similes 145

Let's read: Answer pre-reading questions; explain and justify opinions; inference; devise lower, middle and higher order comprehension questions 147

Grammar builder: Sketch a visual response to a text; annotate with precise and vivid nouns, adjectives, verbs, similes 149

Let's write: Write a story following a story structure diagram; write in paragraphs; re-read, check and edit 150

Project 18: Sound and light in movies 152

Speaking and listening: Listen to a piece of music and sketch a visual response; share opinions, use class communication protocol; listen for rhythm and pitch 152

Word builder: List and categorise topic words; match definitions to words; prefixes, suffixes and root words; spelling strategies; devise and play word games 153

Let's read: Identify viewpoint; persuasive techniques 154

Grammar builder: Similes; parts of speech; comparing and contrasting words; synonyms 156

Let's write: Write a movie or music review; express viewpoint; write in paragraphs 157

Term 2 Unit 1 Review and assessment 159

Term 2 **Unit 2**

The human body system

Project 19: The way we move 162

Speaking and listening: Discuss images of the body; demonstrate the body movements, including verbal and non-verbal elements 162

Word builder: Vocabulary about the human body; syllabification; use technical vocabulary in sentences; etymology 163

Let's read: Use a 3-2-1 table to respond to a text; back up ideas and opinions with evidence; use evidence to evaluate texts; understand the purpose of a text 165

Grammar builder: Demonstrative pronouns and adjectives 167

Let's write: Plan and write a story using an opening stimulus and on a given theme; use the RAFT strategy to identify role, audience, format and topic 168

Project 20: Be strong and healthy 169

Speaking and listening: Read aloud; watch and listen to advertisements and discuss persuasive techniques; hold a class discussion; evaluate and make judgements 169

Word builder: Contractions; common errors; plurals, possessives and contractions 170

Let's read: Analyse advertisements; evaluate audience; discuss opinions; re-write advertisements 171

Grammar builder: Pronouns; singular and plural reflexive pronouns 173

Let's write: Create a visual advertisement for a magazine; write a script for a radio advertisement; write an advertisement which appears to be objective; write for different audiences; use formal/informal language; slogans, opinions, rhymes and alliteration 175

Project 21: They overcame 177

Speaking and listening: Interpret and discuss visual image; agree class response 177

Word builder: Write pronunciation guide; using a dictionary; make a glossary; identify and use spelling strategies 178

Let's read: Middle and higher order comprehension; justify opinions; identify and undertake follow-up research; use RAFT strategy to plan a speech 179

Grammar builder: Subordinate clauses; relative pronouns; relative clauses 182

Let's write: Use the plan in "Research and study skills" lesson to write a speech; use an editing checklist 183

Project 22: The kidneys are amazing organs 184

Speaking and listening: Listen to and answer questions on a text; identify key information points; using the 3-2-1 strategy 184

Word builder: Identify basic and unusual spelling patterns; draw and label a diagram using technical vocabulary; focus on accurate, scientific vocabulary 186

Let's read: Metacognition and thinking strategies; use reading response symbols 187

Grammar builder: Appositive nouns and phrases; punctuation in phrases with appositive phrases; write appositive phrases for technical vocabulary 189

Let's write: Work in groups to plan and prepare a class presentation 190

Project 23: When we need medical help 191

Speaking and listening: Informal discussion using class communications protocol; ask and answer questions; use KWI prompt to support listening and reflection; listen to and discuss a news report 191

Word builder: Vocabulary beginning with chr-; find definitions, use words in context; pronunciation of 'ch' in words 192

Let's read: Read a formal letter using the RAFT strategy; use reading response symbols; share strategies for decoding meaning; identify and explain the purpose of emotional techniques 193

Grammar builder: Identify use of tenses in formal letters; continuous tense and perfect tense; identify signal words and phrases 195

Let's write: Plan and write a formal letter; use signal words, formal style and appropriate technical vocabulary 196

Project 24: Understanding puberty 197

Speaking and listening: Class discussion; use language techniques to support sensitive discussions; listen to and discuss poetry 197

Word builder: Identify syllable pattern and rhythm in words; root words, prefixes and suffixes; define and use accurate technical vocabulary in context 199

Let's read: Pre-reading activities and prediction; call-and-response reading; understand Shakespearean writing; "Let's read" skills 200

Grammar builder: Use speech bubbles, scripts, direct quotation and reported speech; write dialogue; convert quotation to reported speech 202

Let's write: Write a dialogue, a script or a poem on the unit theme 203

Term 2 Unit 2 Review and assessment ... 204

Term 3 Unit 1
Diversity, sustainability and interdependence

Project 25: A diverse country 207

Speaking and listening: Discuss with a partner and a group; compare likes and dislikes; explore differences and similarities ... 207

Word builder: Sort words into categories; use dictionaries or glossaries; discuss symbolism of words 208

Let's read: Read maps and charts; interpret and summarise diagrams; explain patterns in graphs; evaluate non-verbal forms of information 209

Grammar builder: Continuous and perfect verb forms; verb-subject agreement; verb forms with collective nouns 211

Let's write: Evaluate a piece of writing, identifying language choices; research statistical information and write a written interpretation 213

Project 26: Ancestors and descendants ... 215

Speaking and listening: Listen to texts for information; compare and contrast; discuss in groups 215

Word builder: Syllabification, prefixes, suffixes and root words to learn, understand and remember vocabulary; create and participate in spelling challenges 217

Let's read: Understand the difference between personal and formal letters; identify how feelings are expressed in text 218

Grammar builder: Understand the purpose of punctuation marks colon, ellipses, dashes and brackets 219

Let's write: Plan and write a personal letter .. 220

Project 27: Reflecting on colonisation 221

Speaking and listening: Listen to and read a poem aloud; identify characteristics of a poem; articulate a response to poetry; make connections with other artforms 221

Word builder: Onomatopoeic words 223

Let's read: Read and respond to a poem; interpret a poem in actions; write in poetic style; understand the context and setting of a poem; research poet's biography 224

Grammar builder: Reflexive pronouns; punctuation; use a graphic organiser to structure a paragraph 227

Let's write: Compose a poem on a given subject; use poetic techniques 228

Project 28: Ethnic groups 229

Speaking and listening: Prepare interview questions on a given theme; role play interviewing and being interviewed; develop and express knowledge, empathy and understanding 229

Word builder: Inference; syllabification; root words; pronunciation; compile word lists and sample sentences; synonyms 230

Let's read: Read information on a website; answer "Let's read" questions; use inference; identify further research 231

Grammar builder: Contractions; apostrophe of omission and possession; false homophones 233

Let's write: Plan, research and write a presentation on a chosen theme; use notes and visual representations in writing 234

Project 29: The Caribbean 235

Speaking and listening: Ask and answer questions about a map; conduct a class discussion; listen to songs and poems 235

Word builder: Create a Caribbean-themed alphabet; proper nouns; common nouns; adjectives; spelling and pronunciation strategies 236

Let's read: Identify text type from visual appearance, style and tone; summarise; use inference; KWL strategy; evaluate content; explain and justify an opinion 237

Grammar builder: Use of punctuation; format of formal writing; main and subordinate clauses; verb tenses and agreement; devise a presentation on a grammar topic; write instructions; record notes in form of journal 239

Let's write: Plan and compose a formal email 240

Project 30: Shared experiences 241

Speaking and listening: Prepare and deliver a presentation to the class in groups; ask and answer questions; summarise learning points 241

Word builder: Abbreviations and acronyms... 242

Let's read: Read a non-fiction text and answer questions; research and discuss related content; describe meaning; evaluate text 243

Grammar builder: Linking phrases; write linking phrases showing balance between two ideas; use linking phrases in practice debate 245

Let's write: Plan and write a formal speech on a given subject; distinguish between factual evidence and statements of opinion.. 246

Term 3 Unit 1 Review and assessment 247

TERM 1 — Unit 1

Project 1

 **Speaking and listening**

JAMAICA CELEBRATES INDEPENDENCE

1. In groups, discuss what you think the images show. Ask each other questions about the event. For example: *When do you think this happened?*

2. Listen whilst your teacher reads aloud the short description of these events on the next page. Cover the text, listen and make some notes about the account. When you make notes, you do not have time to write full sentences; write key words that will help you remember the details later.

Remember ★ ☆ ☆

Be a good listener:
- Picture the story in your mind.
- Avoid distractions.
- Listen for thoughts and feelings sensitively.

Project 1 – An independent country

When Jamaica gained its independence on 6 August 1962, it was cause for sheer joy, optimism and national pride. At the stroke of midnight, the British Union Jack was lowered and the black, green and gold Jamaican flag was raised for the first time.

In addition to the flag raising, the ceremony (which began at 11 p.m. on 5 August) also featured a national parade and fireworks. There were approximately 20,000 people in attendance at the National Stadium, it was reported. Present were Sir Kenneth Lightbourne, Jamaica's first governor general, his wife, Lady Lightbourne, and Jamaica's premier, Sir Alexander Bustamante, who was later sworn in as Prime Minister. Also, there were Princess Margaret, representing the Queen of England, and her husband, the Earl of Snowdon. Dignitaries from other countries such as the United States, Australia and Pakistan witnessed the ceremony.

3   Discuss the questions in pairs or small groups.

1   **What** is the main point of the account?

2   **When** did it occur?

3   **Who** was involved?

4   **Where** did it happen?

5   **Why** was it important?

Extra challenge

Do you already know some information or some stories from this time? Share these with the class by preparing a short presentation of what you know.

ICT opportunity

You could find out more about this event by using a search engine. Type one or more key words to search for relevant websites. You can find old newspaper reports to read about it.

Remember, you must be sensible when you are online. In pairs, complete the challenge:

- Use a search engine such as Google to search for information on safety rules for children using the internet. Write down three of these rules.
- Compare your answers with the YouTube website by searching for videos titled *Five Internet Safety Tips for Kids*.

Term 1 Unit 1

Word builder

Vocabulary box

independent	government	culture
independence	Britain	reign
country	pre-independence	sovereign
history	post-independence	prehistory

1 Read the words from the vocabulary box with a partner and complete the table. Are there any words you do not know?

I know the meaning and how to say them.	I can read them, but I do not know what they mean.	I am not sure how to pronounce them or what they mean.

ICT opportunity

Use an online dictionary to find the meanings of any words you do not know. Many online dictionaries play a recording of the word to show how to pronounce them, too.

2 The words *government* and *reign* have a silent letter each. Can you find them?

3 Look at the words *pre-independence* and *post-independence*. What is the same and what is different about the words?

Prefix	Meaning	Word example	Word meaning
pre-	before	pre-independence	before independence
post-	after	post-independence	after independence

12

Project 1 – An independent country

Extra challenge

Use a dictionary or another research source to find other words that use the prefixes pre- and post-. See if you can write sentences using these new words.

Remember ☆☆☆

A **prefix** is the part of a word added to the start to change its meaning or form a new word. Can you think of any other prefixes?

Let's read

1 Read the text below and answer the following questions.

Jamaica – A quick guide to an independent country

If you are coming to visit Jamaica, you will be interested to learn a little about this beautiful country and its proud history. In 1962, Jamaica became an independent country. Read this article to find out more about it:

Prehistory

Did you know that there have been people living on Jamaica for 6000 years? But, of course, the country was not named Jamaica in 4000 BC. The Jamaican National Heritage Trust is researching to find out more about the people who lived here before sailors from Europe arrived.

Pre-independence Jamaica

In 1494, Christopher Columbus sailed to Jamaica and it became a colony of Spain. After some years of Spanish rule, the country became part of the British Empire, and it remained that way until 1962.

Post-independence Jamaica

In 1962, Jamaica was declared a sovereign nation. This meant that for the first time in hundreds of years, the country ruled itself. There were great celebrations on the streets and all over the country.

A symbol of independence

You may be surprised to find out that Jamaica did not have its own flag before 1962. Although we have become used to seeing the flag draped around the shoulders of athletes, or flying from the flagpoles on government buildings, it was only raised for the first time on Independence Day.

This Jamaican flag was first raised on Independence Day in August 1962.

Geography facts
- Jamaica is the fourth largest island-nation in the Caribbean.
- It has over 1000 km of coastline.
- There are approximately two and a half million inhabitants in Jamaica.
- Tourism, mining and agriculture are important to the Jamaican economy.

1. Where might you find a text like this in your everyday life? Give two examples.

2. Which headings would you look for to find out about Jamaica before independence?

3. What do we call the sentence that introduces the main point of the paragraph?

4. Do you think that this text would be useful for visitors to Jamaica? Explain why.

Extra challenge

Find all the sentences with the vocabulary from the "Word builder" activity. Are they nouns, verbs or adjectives in this context?

Research and study skills

Text features help organise information in a text so readers know what is important.

1. Copy and complete this table.

Text feature	Purpose	Example in the text
Heading		
Introduction		
Bulleted list		
Caption		

> When I answer comprehension questions, I often **skim** the text first. This means quickly reading to see how the text is organised. Then, when I need to find some information, I **scan** through to find the particular part I need.

2 Summarise the most important information from the text *Jamaica – A quick guide to an independent country*. Use the text features to guide you as you skim and scan the text for the information you need.

3 Who is the intended audience? Use evidence from the text to support your answer.

4 Which aspect do you find most interesting? Describe what you would like to find out more about and the different ways you would do your research.

> Did you know that websites are not always accurate? Before a book is published, many people check to make sure there are no errors and that the information is accurate. For some websites, there are people who check and edit, but anyone can publish a website without any checks at all.

Project 1 – An independent country

Grammar builder

Remember ☆ ☆ ☆

A noun is a part of speech. A noun names an object like *cat, dog, table, chair*. Find the nouns in this sentence:
The old horse lived in a stable.
The nouns which name objects we can sense, point to or touch are called **concrete nouns**.

L👀k and learn

Now we are ready to learn about a different kind of noun: abstract nouns. These are names for ideas or feelings. The words still name something, but you cannot touch them or point to them. For example: angry. You can point to someone who is angry or describe examples of anger, but you could never pick up anger and put it on the table or hide it under your hat!

1 *Kelly's anger burst just like Mike's balloon.* There is a concrete noun and an abstract noun in this sentence. Can you find them both?

2 Complete this mind map as a class for the abstract noun *anger*. Then choose some other abstract nouns from the table to create your own mind maps.

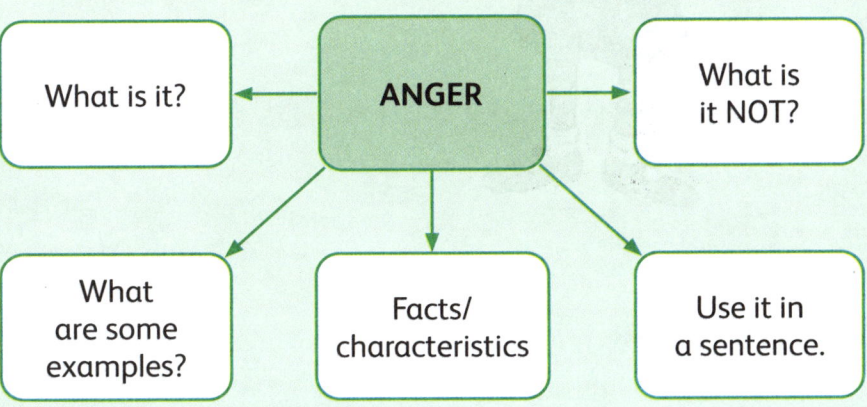

Abstract nouns for feelings	Abstract nouns for ideas
love, fear, hope, happiness	freedom, luck, fairness, independence

Extra challenge

Look at the vocabulary box in the "Word builder" lesson again. Complete a mind map for the abstract noun *culture*.

Project 1 – An independent country

Let's write

This term, we hope to hear some stories from people who have lived in Jamaica for a long time and who can tell us about how it has changed and some of the things that make it so special.

We are going to write letters to people who may remember what it was like to live before and after Jamaica gained independence. We will ask if they could give us an account of what it was like to live through those times and about how it has changed.

Remember ☆☆☆

Look at this example of a letter.

```
                                        Address and date

Dear Mr Hall, ...




Yours sincerely,
Mary
```

You will need to use these layout features in your own letter:
- Address and date
- Dear …

Remember ☆☆☆

Paragraph 1	Paragraph 2	Paragraph 3
Introduce yourself. Ask a polite question. Explain briefly why you are writing.	Describe what you have already learned.	Politely ask for the information you want to find out.

- Yours sincerely or Yours faithfully

19

1. Think about who you will write to and what you want to learn about before you start your letter. Here are some ideas.

I will write to my grandmother. I will ask if she can send us some photographs.

I will write to my next-door neighbour. I will ask if he could come to talk to the class.

Writer's checklist

This is the first writing task of Grade 6. Remember to think about:
- layout
- paragraphs
- style and vocabulary.

What decisions do you need to make before writing a letter?

2. Ask your partner to read your work afterwards. Tell each other one thing that is done well and one thing that can be improved. Make sure you are kind and your comments are useful.

Project 2

Speaking and listening

1. Use information from books or other research options to prepare for a class debate about Jamaican culture. The debate will be on this statement:

   Jamaica's culture is richer now than it was before independence.

   Before you begin, copy this Venn diagram into your notebooks and add a few details from your research into the diagram.

   - What are the differences between Jamaican culture before and after independence?
   - What stayed the same?

   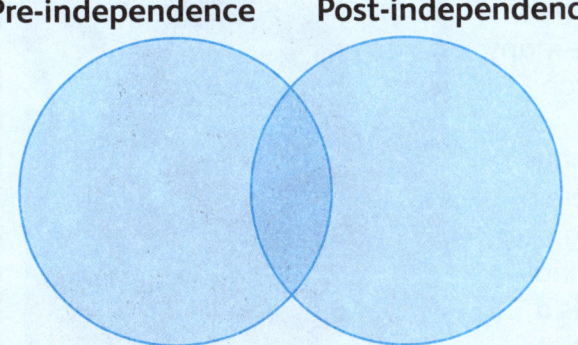

2. Decide whether you will be arguing for the statement or against it. Skim through your research in Activity 1 and use your Venn diagram to remind yourself of the main facts to support your argument.

   ### Remember ☆☆☆

   To take part in an effective debate, you should agree to follow some rules about how to talk and listen to each other. This is called a **communication protocol**.

   The main things to remember are:
   - Listen carefully to what everyone says.
   - Ask questions at an appropriate time.
   - Form your speech clearly and accurately so everyone can understand.
   - If you disagree, say so politely and explain why.

3. After the debate, write an entry for your journal explaining if you heard anything that changed your mind, or if you still have any questions that you want to find out about.

Term 1 Unit 1

Word builder

Vocabulary box

heritage	diversity	religion	theatre
inherited	belief	tradition	generation
literature	stereotype	communities	inhabitants

1 Read the text; there are words in the text that are misspelt. Find the correct word in the vocabulary box and correct each spelling error.

> The cultural heritige of Jamaica includes litarature from great authors and a rich tradision of music. However, there are many stereotipes about Jamaican culture. For example, the Rastafarian religon is famous around the world, but there is a wider divercity among the inhabitents of the island. In fact, modern Jamaica is a blend of beleifs and practices passed down among comunities, inhereted from one generashun to another.

2 Read the passage to your partner. Discuss any meanings you are not sure of. Look at the sentences the words are in to see if you can work out their meaning.

3 Choose three of the words and create a mind map for each in your notebooks.

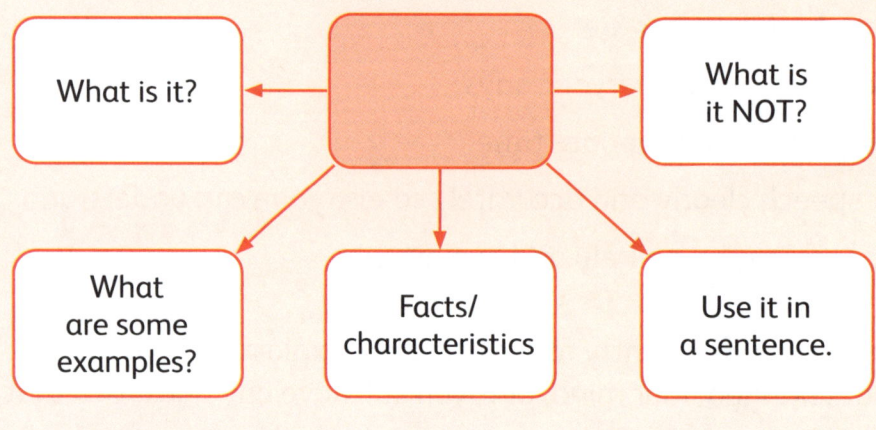

Let's read

1. How much do you know about the national heroes of Jamaica? Read the extracts from the *Jamaica National Heritage Trust* website and then answer the questions that follow.

Fast facts – National heroes

Nanny of the Maroons

Nanny of the Maroons is the only national heroine in Jamaica. She is remembered for the inspiration she gave to her people in fighting the English oppressors in the early 18th century.

Nanny was a leader of her village, Nanny Town, in the parish of Portland, Jamaica.

According to Beverley Carey's The Maroon Story, Nanny died between 1758 –1762.

Legend has it that she possessed superhuman powers.

Source: http://www.jnht.com/fast_facts_national_heroes.php

Samuel "Sam" Sharpe

Samuel Sharpe, also called *Daddy Sharpe*, was a Deacon at the Burchell Baptist Church in Montego Bay. He spent most of his time travelling to different estates in St James educating the slaves about Christianity and freedom. Sharpe had formed a Secret Society among the slaves and many of his meetings were held at night. In 1831, he led the Christmas Rebellion, which started at Kensington Estate in St James and then spread throughout the western end of the island.

Source: http://www.jnht.com/fast_facts_national_heroes.php

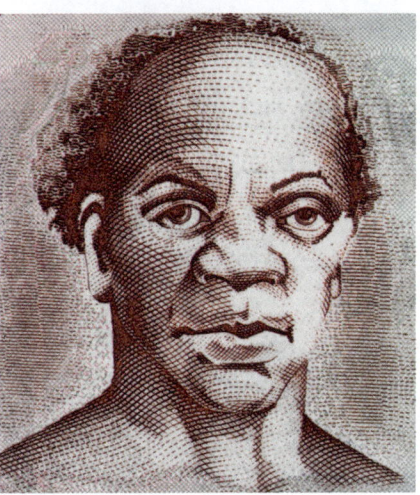

Emancipation and independence

We hold celebrations every year to commemorate emancipation and independence. This allows us to explore different aspects of our culture and to reflect on who we are. In this way we develop a better understanding of our history and culture.

1. Whose date of death is not known exactly?

2. It says Nanny was an *inspiration*. Find the sentence and explain what the word *inspiration* means in this context.

3. Nanny possessed superhuman powers: True or false? Explain your reasoning.

4. Samuel and Nanny shared a common cause. Explain this sentence.

5. Write three questions you would ask each national hero.

6. The Independence Celebrations are described as important. Explain the reasons given for this in the text.

Research and study skills

1. With your partner, discuss what you already know about national heroes and what you would like to find out about them. Think about ways you could do more research. What clues are there in the texts above to help you find out more?

Look and learn

Each extract from the *Fast facts – National heroes* has a source that shows exactly where the information is published. This is very important because if you reuse any information from the original source, you need to give credit to the original authors. It also allows the reader to research further and to decide how accurate the information is.

2.
1. Visit the *Jamaican National Heritage Trust* website and other online sources. With your partner, research a national hero. Skim passages for main ideas and decide how this hero has contributed to Jamaican independence or Jamaican culture.

2. Collect a set of references that you will use for research. Make a note of useful page numbers by using the contents and index, or by using the alphabetical order of an encyclopaedia.

3 Create a mind map to organise your notes as you collect them, with your headings arranged so you can note facts and other points of interest.

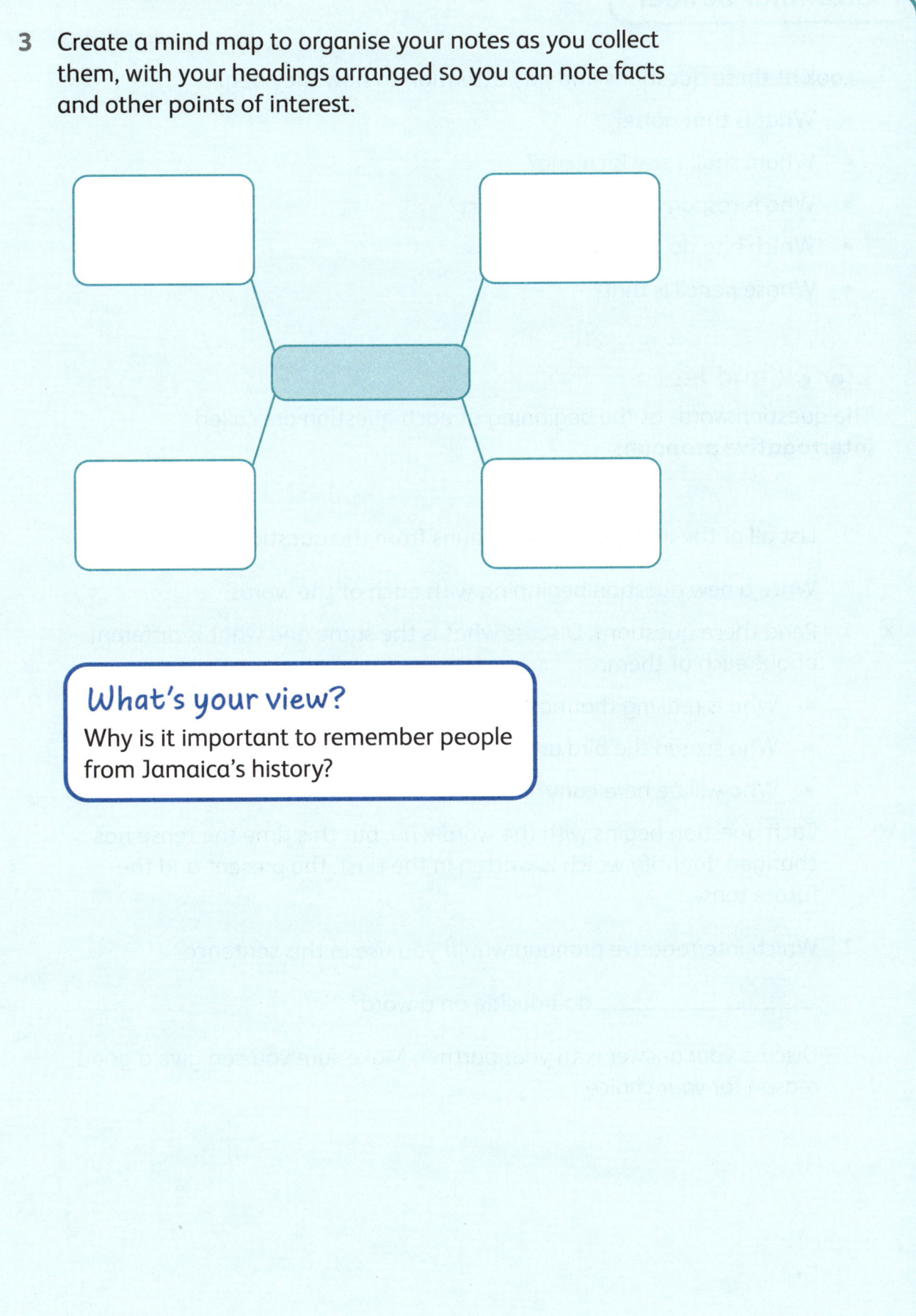

What's your view?
Why is it important to remember people from Jamaica's history?

Grammar builder

1 Look at these questions and pay attention to how they begin:
- What is that noise?
- Whom shall I say is calling?
- Who is responsible for this project?
- Which bag do you prefer?
- Whose pencil is that?

Look and learn

The question words at the beginning of each question are called **interrogative pronouns**.

1. List all of the interrogative pronouns from the questions above.
2. Write a new question beginning with each of the words.

2 1 Read these questions. Discuss what is the same and what is different about each of them.
- Who is making that noise?
- Who scared the bird away?
- Who will be here early?

Each question begins with the word *who*, but this time the tense has changed. Identify which is written in the past, the present and the future tense.

2 Which interrogative pronoun would you use in this sentence?

_____ do I decide on a word?

Discuss your answer with your partner. Make sure you can give a good reason for your choice.

3 Complete the table using the correct tenses.

	Past	Present	Future
What	What were the songs?	What are the songs?	What will be the songs?
Who		Who sings in the choir?	
Whom			To whom will I speak?
Which	Which did you select?		
Whose		Whose house is this?	

Extra challenge

Write a question beginning with each of these words. What do you notice about the tenses you have to use?

Did   Do   Does   Were   Are   Will

Term 1 Unit 1

Let's write

Write a script titled *Pieces from the Past*.

- Write a script to relive an episode from the life of someone living at the moment of independence.
- Think about the language of your characters.

Plan

Use these boxes to plan:

Characters	Setting	Event
		The family prepares for Independence Day celebrations.

Think about how the characters respond to Independence Day celebrations and show it in their speech.

Write

Present your script in the correct format. Look at the example.

Pieces from the Past

Scene: a living room. A grandfather is mending a chair. A young man is dressed smartly.

David: Ah, whey dem did deh?

Grandfather: *(ignores him)* Dis chair …

Perform and review

- Take it in turns to role play your scripts.
- Write a short review of your favourite performance.
- Discuss the use of Jamaican Creole (JC) or Standard Jamaican English (SJE).

28

Project 3 – Then and now

Project 3

Speaking and listening

1. Discuss these photographs. Use clues to put them in order from the earliest to the most recent.

2. In pairs, choose one of the photographs. Imagine that you are in the scene or event. Describe the scene to your partner using Jamaican Creole (JC). Now let your partner describe the same scene using Standard Jamaican English (SJE).

3. Which words did you change? Keep a list and be ready to perform your different versions to the class. See if they can hear the differences. Which version do you prefer to use to describe the scene or event? Why?

Extra challenge

Listen to an account from someone who has experienced the changes after independence. You may have a class visitor, listen to a recording or your teacher may show you a video clip. Think of questions that you could ask the speaker to find out more.

Word builder

1. Read the words from the vocabulary box aloud to your partner. Some of the words are homophones. This means that they sound the same but they have different meanings and are spelt differently.

Vocabulary box

their	hole	weak	heard	tail	two
week	tale	plane	plain	they're	there
too	to	hear	here	whole	
hour	herd	read	red	our	

2. Find the homophones and sort them into two groups. Use a dictionary or discuss with your classmates how to learn the ones you do not know.

I know how to use these correctly.	I am unsure how to use these correctly.

3. Choose one group of homophones and write a sentence to show how to use each word correctly.

4. Look at this text. It has some false homophones. Read it to your partner. When it is read out loud, the words sound correct, but some mistakes have been made.

> I love my too Ants. Dey came over to hour manner and brought dear dog. I got too baby-sit de dog, scents dey were flying on a plain to a mountain peek for a ski trip. I got along well with dear dog while it stayed with me, and he had a good time, even though he was scratching and trying two flea from his flees. My mom was angry, dough, when he stuck his knows and pause into the desert bowl, then left read paw prints on the carpet. He wags his tale every mourning when he wakes up to show dat he is happy. He stayed a hole weak, and he did not even brake a thing.

1. Identify all the mistakes and rewrite them using the correct homophones. The first ten are highlighted for you.

2. Check your work with your partner. Have you both correctly identified the homophones? Are there any you missed? Why do you think that is? Can you think of a way to remember them next time?

Let's read

1 Read the extracts which give details about some of the events leading up to independence and the years after independence. Then answer the questions that follow.

Marcus Garvey

Born the youngest of 11 children, Marcus Garvey did a great deal to promote civil rights in the early decades of the 20th century. He led strikes for improved pay, before speaking in America and around the world to promote the rights of black people in Jamaica and other countries. Since then, he has become an inspirational figure in the history of civil rights and was declared the first National Hero of Jamaica.

The Great Depression

In the 1930s, Jamaica suffered economic hardship, just like the USA and the rest of the world. The price of sugar dropped sharply and there was low employment, low wages, hunger and hardship. There were riots and widespread violence in 1938, which prompted further strikes and a demand for action.

Votes for the people

In 1944, one year before the end of World War II, the Universal Adult Suffrage was announced. This meant that all Jamaicans over the age of 21 could vote in elections. After this, in December 1944, the first election under Universal Suffrage was held, and Jamaica began on the path to independence.

Post-independence

In the years after 1962, further reforms were introduced. Free education beyond primary level was provided for all. This meant many people had the chance to be qualified for better-paid jobs. Equal pay for women was also introduced. Following that was the right to maternity leave. Furthermore, the voting age was lowered to 18.

1. List any words that confuse you or that you have not heard before. Write some suggestions for what they could mean. Remember to use clues from the sentence and the paragraphs they are in.

2. Do you think that one of these events was more important in Jamaican history than the others? Discuss your ideas in groups.

3. Draw a timeline with your partner to show the order of the main events described in the extracts. Add any other events that you have discovered from your research. Even if you are not sure of the exact year, you should be able to place your events in the correct order.

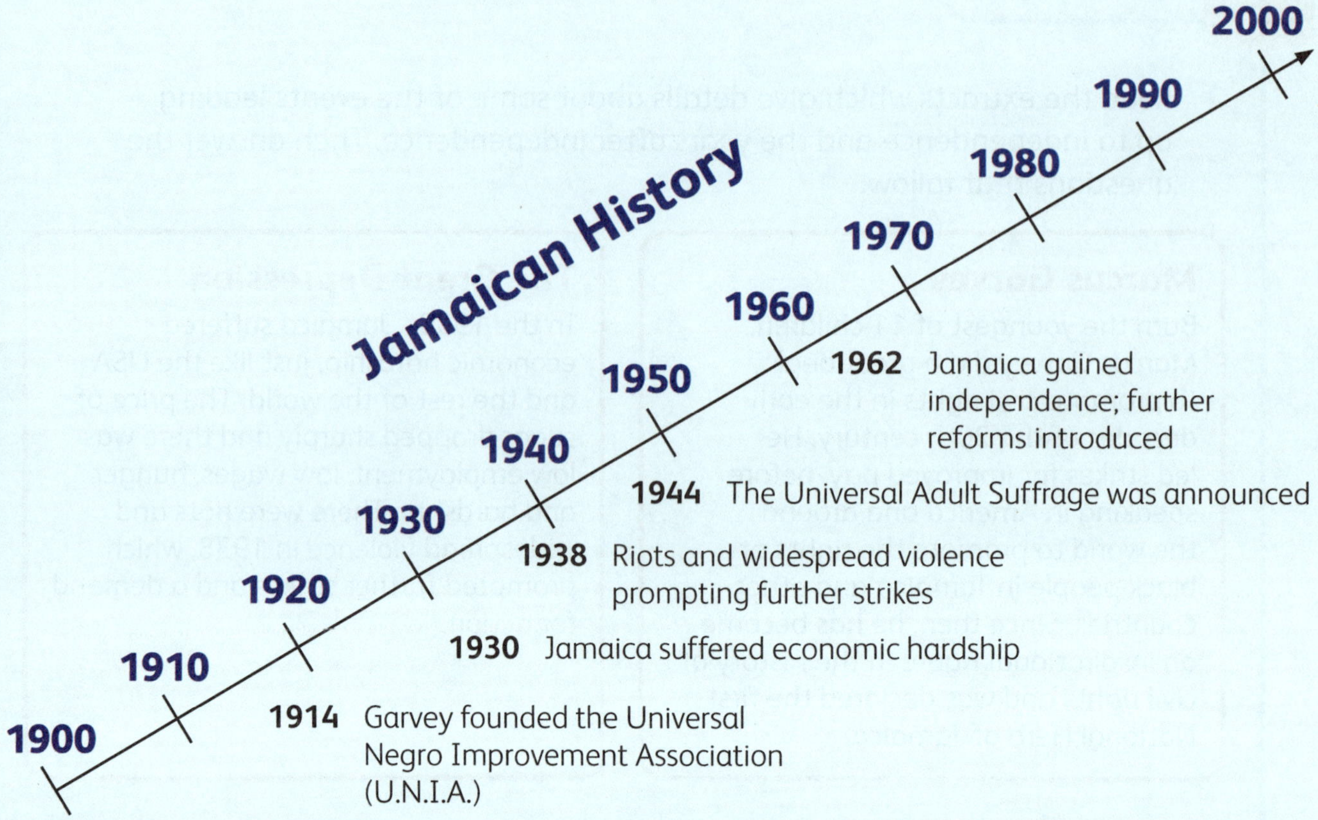

Jamaican History
1900
1910
1920
1930
1940
1950
1960
1970
1980
1990
2000
1962 Jamaica gained independence; further reforms introduced
1944 The Universal Adult Suffrage was announced
1938 Riots and widespread violence prompting further strikes
1930 Jamaica suffered economic hardship
1914 Garvey founded the Universal Negro Improvement Association (U.N.I.A.)

A timeline of Jamaican history from 1900 to 2000.

Research and study skills

1 Make a copy of the Venn diagram in your notebook.

Pre-independence
Post-independence

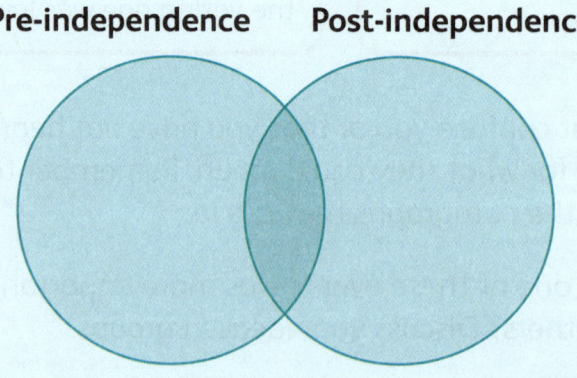

1. Think about what you know already about life in pre- and post-independence Jamaica. What aspects of life, culture, work and politics have changed since 1962, and what has stayed the same?

2. Add any aspects to the Venn diagram. Here are some areas to think about:
   - voting and government
   - jobs and employment
   - culture and identity
   - family and home life
   - how Jamaica is viewed by the rest of the world.

> **Extra challenge**
>
> From further research using ICT, books, visits to heritage centres or speaking to people who were alive to experience the changes, what further details can you add to the Venn diagram?

2. Share your ideas with a partner or in a group. Between you, decide on the key aspects of how life has changed. It will be interesting to see if you agree or disagree about any of the changes.

3. Work as a group to present your ideas to the class. Decide on the main points that you would like to share from your Venn diagram. Decide which are the most interesting and explain why in your presentation. Make sure that everyone has a turn.

When speaking, make sure that:
   - everyone has a turn speaking
   - you say why you chose your main points
   - you state the changes and the similarities.

When listening to other students' presentations, remember to:
   - make notes of any interesting ideas
   - wait until the end of the presentation to ask a question.

Grammar builder

These linking words and phrases can be used at the beginning of a sentence to link it with the rest of the paragraph and with the idea that came before.

Here are three categories of linking phrases:

Time sequence	Additional	Contrasting
before that	also	but
next	similarly	however
then	likewise	despite that
after that		yet
afterwards		

1. Use three of the sequencing words to write instructions for how to make a good impression when you start in a new class at school. Think carefully about the order you would do things in. You may also use your own linking words in your instructions, but add them to the correct category in the table.

2. Write about the similarities and differences between you and your partner, using the "Additional" and "Contrasting" link phrases. Make sure you are kind! Discuss your work afterwards. Did you point out the same similarities and differences? Did you use similar linking words?

3. Decide which category the following linking words should be in:

    1. following that
    2. yet
    3. despite that
    4. furthermore
    5. in addition

4. Use each linking word above in sentences about something that happened in your class, your school or your family.

Extra challenge

Write a short story. Start each sentence with the linking words *since*, *then* and *while*. Swap stories with a partner and ask him or her to replace the linking words with different ones. Challenge your partner to improve your story while you try to improve theirs.

Project 3 – Then and now

Let's write

Write a journal entry, recording the main aspects in which life in Jamaica has changed from pre-independence to post-independence.

- This should be at least a paragraph and should include some of the linking words and phrases you learned in this project.
- Include a copy of the Venn diagram you created in the "Research and study skills" section to complete your journal entry. You might want to change some of the details after you have listened to everybody's presentations.

Editor's checklist

Check you have included:
- linking words and phrases for comparisons
- accurate vocabulary
- correct homophones.

Project 4

Speaking and listening

Listen to your teacher read aloud these short news items from 15 February 1962. These are stories from the time just before independence.

The Jamaican Weekly Gleaner
15 February 1962

Premier Norman Manley and Opposition Leader Sir Alexander Bustamante raised the roof during the plenary session at Lancaster House in the United Kingdom during talks to determine the date of Jamaica's Independence Day.

Sir Alexander Bustamante banged the table, rolled up his sleeves, got red in the face and raged loudly that if Her Majesty's government thought they could deceive the people of Jamaica they were mistaken, for there would be rebellion if Britain tried to keep Jamaica back from Independence by even one date beyond the day asked.

Gleaner vehicle stolen

A vehicle stolen from The Gleaner Company was recovered in the vicinity of Blake Road by traffic police. The van, which was abandoned, was apparently undamaged when recovered. No arrest was made in connection with the theft.

Bread-price warning

A warning has been given by the Hon Wills Isaacs, minister of trade and industry, that bread will be put under control if there is any attempt to increase the price.

1. As you listen make notes:
   - What happened?
   - What caused it to happen?
2. After listening, discuss these questions with your partner:
   - Who was in the news?
   - Where did the stories take place?
   - What happened?
   - What sort of news stories were they?
   - Were there any words you were unsure of?
3. With your partner, write three questions in your notebook to ask the class, one for each text. Make a note of the likely answers.

Project 4 – It was in the news

Word builder

Vocabulary box

unclear	declutter	disorganise	misremembered
misused	unsure	deform	distrust
displace	misplaced	unloved	deflate

1. Read the words from the vocabulary box and find the four different prefixes. Use an example from the words to complete the table below for each prefix. Discuss with your partner what each prefix does to the word you attach it to.

Prefix	Meaning	Word example	Word meaning
un-			
mis-			

2. Think of your own example of a word for each of the prefixes. Challenge yourself or your partner to put them into a sentence.

3. Choose three of the words and use them in a short story. Now change the story by removing all the prefixes. Read both versions to your partner. Did the story make sense?

4. Read this news story, which is told by one of the local children who witnessed the events. Identify the false homophones and rewrite it in Standard Jamaican English (SJE).

Dey was dis auto vehicle by de said of de rode and we didn't sea it until two day. I guess dat it was stolen from de news paper the day be four or even be for dat. I was a bit scarred but I wanted to peak in too sea if the teeth had left be hind any evidents but I couldn't fined anything. I wander watt happened?

Extra challenge

Write a different witness account about the news story. Write it in Jamaican Creole (JC) with some false homophones. Challenge a partner to rewrite it in Standard Jamaican English (SJE).

Let's read

Read this report about a different news item, which also took place on 15 February 1962. Then complete the tasks that follow.

> **Telephone emergency**
>
> Yesterday, the Jamaica Telephone Company had to send more workers out to repair the telephone wires along the north coast. This was due to further damage of lines which many say is related to the ongoing strike.
>
> It is reported that the telephone lines are deliberately being cut. The JTC blame striking workers. There have been as many as 1,300 workers taking part in the strike, which has continued into its fifth day. The chief engineer of the company has said that the damage amounts to "sabotage".
>
> The damage to the telephone wires has left many areas isolated. These areas include Ocho Rios, Tower Isle and Lucea. Residents of these areas have been unable to make telephone contact with the rest of Jamaica. Some have been concerned that this will cause an issue in the case of emergency in the affected areas.
>
> As of yet, there is no sign of the strike being resolved.

1. Read the following sentences and decide whether they are true or false.

    1. Telephone wires fell down in a storm.
    2. Engineers repaired the damaged lines.
    3. The telephone damage caused a strike.
    4. The whole of Jamaica was affected.

2. Read the headline again. Some residents were concerned about what would happen in an emergency. Explain how the damage could cause a problem.

3. Suggest what caused the damage to the lines. Does the article give a definite reason?

4. Describe three or more consequences of the damage to the lines.

5. Many newspapers interview people and report what they have said in their articles. In this article, the chief engineer of the JTC was interviewed. Think of two more people that could have been interviewed for this article, and explain why they would be suitable choices.

6. Headlines help to grab the reader's attention and tell them what the article is about in a few words. Think of another headline that could be used for this article.

Extra challenge

Find the words *sabotage* and *resolved* in the news story. Use the context of the sentences and the news report to suggest accurate definitions for each word. Write a sentence with each of the words to show how they can be used properly.

Grammar builder

Paragraphs need to be organised so that their meaning is clear and the reader's attention is drawn to the most important message.

Look at this diagram:

Opening sentence → Supporting details → Concluding sentence

1. In groups, discuss what is important for each different aspect:
   - Opening sentences need to be …
   - The supporting details should …
   - A good concluding sentence must …

2. Rearrange these fragments in order to make a paragraph.

   Tip: Look for the opening and concluding sentences first.

   1. The vehicle was finally returned to its rightful owners.
   2. The police were unable to collect much evidence because nothing had been damaged.
   3. An unexplained crime has been partly solved by a local boy.
   4. However, it was spotted by a local boy when he was playing with his friends.
   5. A vehicle was stolen from the offices of *The Gleaner* some time on Tuesday night.
   6. The newspaper presumed it would not be seen again.

3. Based on your group discussions in Activity 1, rewrite the opening and concluding sentences to be more effective.

Let's write

Imagine you are the reporter who uncovered the truth about a mystery stolen car.

You are going to use the following stages of the writing process to produce a report:

- plan main ideas
- plan paragraphs
- add details
- check and edit.

Plan main ideas

Decide on the truth behind the reasons for the car being stolen but not damaged. Perhaps it was all a big misunderstanding. Or perhaps it was used as a rescue vehicle, or to help in an emergency. Discuss ideas with a partner.

Plan paragraphs

Think of how to organise your report. There will be five paragraphs: an introduction, three body paragraphs and a conclusion. Complete the table to plan your writing.

- First, write an opening sentence for each body paragraph.

Paragraph	Opening sentence
Introduction	
Paragraph 1 – Recap the news of the mystery car.	
Paragraph 2 – Explain the events that helped solve the mystery.	
Paragraph 3 – Describe effects on the people involved.	
Conclusion	

Add details

- Now add the detail sentences to each paragraph. Include conjunctions and linking phrases to show the cause and effect.

Check and edit

- Once it is complete, check through it with a partner. Can you identify the opening, details and concluding sentence of each paragraph? If not, edit your work to show them more clearly.

Project 5

Speaking and listening

1. Look at these pictures. Can you identify the period of history?

2. Answer the following questions.

Factual thinking

1. What would the island have looked like in these times?

2. How would the island have sounded or smelled in these times?

3. What foods do you think would have been common?

4. How would people spend their time?

Project 5 – Stories from the past

Emotional thinking

1. What would it have felt like to be alive in these times?

2. How might different people have experienced it differently?

3. Would you have liked to live in these historical times or do you prefer the present day? Can you explain why?

After you have had some time for quiet reflection on these questions, spend some time listening to each other and make notes of any interesting thoughts that had not occurred to you before.

Extra challenge

Discuss the question: Who discovered Jamaica?
Think carefully about the different possible historical viewpoints.

Word builder

Remember ☆☆☆

Adjectives modify a noun. They are words that give more precise details about a noun.

They can appear before the noun:
The **old** hat couldn't protect him from the **fierce** heat.
Or they can appear after the verb to be:
The hat was **old** and the heat was **fierce**.

Can you find the adjectives in this sentence?
She picked up my favourite book and asked if it was funny.

The suffixes -*ful*, -*less* and -*able* often form adjectives. They can transform nouns or verbs into adjectives:

forget + ful → forgetful

hope + less → hopeless

love + able → lovable

1. Use the words *forgetful*, *hopeless* and *lovable* in a sentence. Explain how the suffixes have added a new meaning to the root words.

2. Experiment with these words. Try adding different suffixes: *heart*, *forgive*, *beauty*, *memory*. You may need to adapt the spelling to add the suffixes. Check the words in a dictionary after you have found the correct suffix for each.

3. Try using the words *fearful*, *thoughtless* and *forgettable* in a sentence or a short paragraph.

4. Swap the sentence or paragraph with your partner. Change the meaning of the sentence by swapping the adjectives around. Now read the new text to your partner. See if it makes them smile!

Extra challenge

Research other words that end with one of these suffixes. Collect a list to share or display in the classroom.

Project 5 – Stories from the past

Let's read

1 Read these texts carefully.

Text A: The Arawaks or Tainos – The first people of the Caribbean

The Arawaks and the Caribs were the first people of the Caribbean. They settled in these islands long before Christopher Columbus arrived in 1494. The Arawaks or the Tainos, as some of them were called, were not tall people; they were of medium height or short and generally slim. Christopher Columbus in his journals described them as neither black nor white. It is believed that they had an olive complexion. They also had long, straight, coarse black hair. For the Arawaks, to be beautiful meant having flattened foreheads, so they would place the head of their babies between two boards and so flatten their foreheads and shape their skulls up to a peak.

The Arawaks were a peaceful people. In fact, the word *Taino* is an Arawak word meaning "peace". Columbus noted that they were very honest and stole nothing from the Spaniards. He also wrote that they were generous and sympathetic. For fun, they had many festivals. They also had religious festivals. During these festivals they had much singing and dancing. Women and men danced separately, but sometimes they danced together to the music of drums, reed pipes and wooden gongs.

Text B: Mountain Pride

Once there walked on this rich soil a young and beautiful woman. So much did her parents admire her, they gave her the name Mountain Pride, for she was indeed as majestic as the slopes of a mountain lit by the low evening sun. But, she was a proud girl too, and planned to marry her Cacique, the leader of her people. What could be more fitting than such a match?

On the day of their wedding, the sun rose and Mountain Pride smiled. This was to be a great day. But a bright sun casts dark shadows, and in one of those shadows lurked a priest who felt himself as worthy as any Cacique. "Cacique!" He spat the word out, so much had he grown to hate the man.

On this very morning, he lurked, hidden along the path he knew the Cacique would walk on his way to the wedding. Just as the Cacique passed, the priest leapt out and murdered him. Now, instead of the Cacique, it was the priest who presented himself to Mountain Pride as her future husband.

But Mountain Pride refused. In the end, her love for the Cacique was even greater than her pride, and she threw herself to her death. At the very spot where she fell, there grew a tree. And since that day, the tree still grows and the bright pink blossoms are the same as the colour of the evening sun.

45

2 Compare and contrast the texts. What types of text are they? How can you tell?

3 What is the main purpose of Text A? Compare that with the purpose of Text B.

4 List three different adjectives used in Text A and three in Text B.

5 Describe the different techniques that the author uses to engage the reader in each text.

6 1 Identify a question used in Text B. Find and copy the question.

    2 The question does not require an answer. Explain why the author has used it in this text.

7 Draw a picture to illustrate each text and write a caption for each illustration. Think about the kinds of illustration that would be most suitable for each type of text.

8 Which text did you find more enjoyable to read? Compare and contrast your ideas with a partner.

Project 5 – Stories from the past

Grammar builder

> **Look and learn**
>
> The **subordinate clause** is the part of a sentence that is headed by the conjunction.
> For example:
> *The Taino were enslaved **because** they could not fight back.*
> The main clause is: *The Taino were enslaved.*
> The subordinate clause is headed by *because*: *they could not fight back.*

1 Read these sentences which are made up of a main and a subordinate clause and complete the following tasks.

When Columbus landed, the Taino had lived on this island for many years.

If the Taino already lived here, then Columbus did not discover this land.

Although the Taino posed no threat, they were enslaved.

  1 Identify the conjunctions in these sentences. Describe the different meanings of the conjunctions.

  2 Each sentence is made from two clauses. Write each sentence separately.

  3 Identify the main clause and the subordinate clause in each sentence.

  4 Rearrange the sentences so that the main clause comes before the subordinate clause. Do not forget that the conjunction must move with the subordinate clause.

2 Complete each sentence by adding a main clause to each.

  1 When the Spanish boats arrived on the shore, …

  2 If Columbus had not arrived, …

  3 Although the waves were high, …

3 Now reverse the order, so the main clause is written before the subordinate clause.

> **Extra challenge**
>
> Try using the conjunctions *unless* and *while* to write sentences with a main clause and a subordinate clause.

47

Let's write

For the next two weeks, you will undertake a writing project. You will use different stages in the writing process. Imagine that you were living in Jamaica when the Spanish boats first landed. Plan and write a first draft about what happens when the boats land and the events that follow.

The Tainos named the island *Xaymaca*, which meant "land of wood and water", and is now known as *Jamaica*.

Planning

- Use the visual organiser to generate some ideas before you begin. Use these headings to jot some ideas for the account you will write.

Who	What	Why	Where	When

- Use pictures from the time of the Taino or information from your reading to list some adjectives that could be used in your story. Think about everything you have learned so far in this unit to help you: sights, sounds, smells, emotions.

- With your partner or as a class, discuss the story techniques that are often used to appeal to readers: characters, openings, suspense, description.

Writing

- Write your first draft. You may decide to use a paragraph planner like the one in the "Let's write" lesson in Project 4. Some people find it useful to write the first sentence of each paragraph and then to fill in the details afterwards.

- Give yourself some time to try out different ideas. Do not feel that it has to be perfect the first time. This is an opportunity to write with some freedom. Share your ideas with a partner, who will ask you questions about your draft story. See what questions he/she asks; perhaps this will lead to a new idea that you can add to your story.

Project 6

Speaking and listening

Listen carefully while your teacher reads this poem by the poet James Berry and complete the tasks on the next page.

Words of a Jamaican Laas Moment Them

When I dead
mek rain fall.
Mek the air wash.
Mek the lan wash
good-good.
Mek dry course
them run, and run.

As laas breath gone
mek rain burst –
hilltop them work
waterfall, and all
the gully them gargle fresh.

Mek breadfruit limb them drip,
mango limb them drip. Cow, hog, fowl
stan still, in the burst of clouds.
Poinciana bloom them soak off, clean-clean.
Grass go unda water.

Instant I gone
mek all the Island wash – wash away
the mess of my shortcomings –
all the brok-up things I did start.
Mi doings did fall short too much.
Mi ways did hurt mi wife too oftn.

by James Berry

Understanding the poem

1. Use these phrases to discuss the poem.
   - I think the main idea is …
   - In my opinion, the writer's purpose was to …
   - A good title would be … because …
2. Are there any questions you want to ask to help understand the poem? List these and share with the class.

Responding to the poem

3. How do you react to this poem?
   - Does this remind you of anyone you know or any feelings you have?
   - Does it paint any pictures or memories for you?

Performing the poem

4. Read the poem with your partner. Try different rhythms, pauses, tones of voice.

- What suits your interpretation best?
- What does not suit it at all?
- Does listening to another person perform the poem give you any new understanding or ideas?

ICT opportunity

There is a recording of the poet James Berry reading and talking about his own poem on the *Poetry Archive* website: https://poetryarchive.org/poet/james-berry/. This is a wonderful opportunity to hear the poet's own interpretations and the rhythms of the language.

Project 6 – Jamaican literature

Word builder

Vocabulary box

memory	forgiveness	regret
emotion	sympathy	hopefulness
description	tolerance	dismay
sensitivity	understanding	remembrance

1. How would you describe the theme of these words? What sort of thing are all the words about?
2. Work with a partner. Test each other's spelling. Afterwards, check your spellings, then make a list of three words that you found most difficult.

Mnemonics

A **mnemonic** is a way of remembering how to spell a word. Here is an example for the word *regret*.

Red

Emotions

Give

Really

Endless

Trouble

3. Create your own mnemonics for the words you found most difficult to spell. Memorise them and teach your favourite to the class.

Extra challenge

Look back through the words you have learned in this unit, including prefixes, suffixes and false homophones. Select a tricky word to spell from each week and create a mnemonic to remember it.

51

Let's read

This is an extract from a version of the story *The Legend of Lovers' Leap*. The story is about a beautiful young woman named Akipele and what happened when she married her love, Ipingele. They were both slaves on a plantation, but when they were to be separated, they decided to marry and escape.

The Legend of Lover's Leap

The new overseer gave the alarm, "Get the dogs, slaves escaping."

Akipele's heart beat fast. It was going so fast you could hear it. She was afraid; if they were caught, that would be the end of them. But they were young and quick; they ran fast through the fields. They headed to the hills. In the distance they could hear the dogs and see the burning torches. They had to keep running. The rocky path cut their bare feet and the bushes lashed their faces.

The dogs were closing in on them fast. They could hear them getting closer. Akipele fell to her knees,and with her hands held hight, prayed, "Dear God, help us." Ipengele urged her on, "Come Akipele, we can pray while we run." No sooner had he spoken than there was a burst of thunder and lightning flashed across the sky. The rain emptied down. A sudden gust of wind took the young couple and hurled them round and round. Grabbing hold of Akipele's hand, Ipengele let the wind take them where it wanted. And just as sudden, everything became still. The wind died down.

The rain stopped. Akipele looked around her, noting that she could no longer hear the dogs. The storm had carried them away from the plantation, the dogs and their hunters. They were atop a beautiful cliff. The sea looked very blue and inviting. "Ipengele, look! The sea, it's our way home."

"Not so fast, my young ones." The voice was sharp.

It was the new plantation owner, pointing a gun at them.

Akipele looked at Ipengele. Ipengele looked at Akipele. Without a word, just holding hands, they jumped. The cliff was high, the fall was steep. Down and down they went, holding hands, their love wrapped tight around them.

"But," my grandmother said, "the story didn't just end there. Two beautiful birds were seen soaring high into the sky after they fell, so who knows?"

And as for the plantation owner, he got into such a rage that suddenly his heart gave out and he crumpled to the ground.

1. What is the main point of this extract? Try to describe its meaning in just one sentence.
2. What are the main events? Draw a road map of the story, using pictures or symbols to represent the main events. Compare them with your partner. Have you chosen the same events? Have you drawn similar pictures? Why or why not? Explain what you chose and why.
3. Describe the similarities and differences with the story *Mountain Pride*. Think about why the stories might be similar and why they might be different.
4. Think about the events of the story. Make a table like the one below to show the causes (something that makes an event happen) and effects (what happens because of the event) in the story. The first one is done for you.

Cause	Effect
Akipele and Ipingele escaped from the plantation.	The overseer let out the dogs and they had to run for their lives.

5. How do you respond to the extract of *The Legend of Lovers' Leap*? What emotions do you feel when you read it?
6. Identify different techniques the author has used, giving examples of the following:

   1. adjectives
   2. dialogue
   3. sound effects
   4. questions.

Extra challenge

There are many versions of this tale. Perhaps you already know one or have heard it told before. Research other versions in books, from storytelling, or with the help of your teacher, online. Compare the similarities and differences.

ICT opportunity

Create a presentation that shows the similarities between the stories *Mountain Pride* and *The Legend of Lovers' Leap*. Why do you think the stories have similarities? You may wish to include images of locations relevant to each story.

Term 1 Unit 1

Grammar builder

> **Remember** ☆☆☆
>
> A **subordinate clause** is a clause that is introduced with a conjunction. There are different types of subordinate clauses. A **relative clause** is introduced with a **relative pronoun**, such as *who*, *which* or *that*.

1 Read the following sentences. Underline the relative clause in each sentence. Read each sentence out loud, but miss out the relative clause.

  1 Sam's leg, which was broken in the accident, has been pinned together.

  2 Sam, who recovered well, can now play football again.

  3 Sam trains on Thursdays, which is convenient.

  4 They play on the pitch that was resurfaced recently.

2 Choose an appropriate relative pronoun to complete the following sentences.

  1 Aaliyah is one of the students _____ studies hardest.

  2 She likes to read _____ her brother watches TV.

  3 The subject _____ she likes best is history.

3 Write sentences using the following relative clauses.

  1 … who was born in 2001

  2 … which always reminds me of my grandmother

  3 … that surprised everyone who saw it

  4 … while preparing for the party

  5 … who did not actually know anything about how to repair engines

4 It is important to make sure that the verb of the relative clause agrees with the subject of the sentence. What is wrong with the following sentence? Find and circle two mistakes. Rewrite the sentence correctly.

The children, who was in the play, all need to learn their lines before the performance.

Project 6 – Jamaican literature

Let's write

1. Let's return to the story you wrote in Project 5. Read through your story again. Think about the questions in the "Editor's checklist". Then answer them. What is the main improvement you would like to make to your story?

> Did you know, every writer or novelist writes many drafts before their stories are complete. Tolstoy was a very famous writer from Russia. His most famous book, *War and Peace*, is over 1000 pages long. He wrote eight drafts before it was published – and this was before computers, so every draft was handwritten!

"This is my chance to improve the story that I began in the last project. Great! Now I can make it even more interesting to read."

Editor's checklist

Whether you have written or typed your work, check it carefully when you finish.

- Is the writing accurate?
- Are the details supported by adjectives?
- Are the paragraphs organised clearly to show the main events?
- How does it engage the reader?

2. Look at this table. It shows different techniques to improve the beginning of a story.

Types of leads	Unexciting example	Exciting example	Version for my story
Talking Begins with dialogue.	There was a problem with the train when I went to visit Grandma.	"Quick! Get away from the window," my brother yelled. "What? What is it?"; my sister's eyes were wide with fear.	
Sound effect An event or a sound that propels the reader into the action of the story.	I liked to play hide and seek in the garden.	Crack! I froze. I could hear my heart beating and feel the air trying to burst from my lungs as I tried to stay as still as a statue.	
Question An interesting question to make the reader think.	This story will tell you about what happened on my trip.	Have you ever looked forward to something so much you thought your heart would burst?	
Flashback Takes the reader back to feel what it was like at a time in the past.			

3. Discuss the difference in effect between an unexciting example and the exciting example. What makes the exciting example more exciting?

4. Choose your favourite technique from the table to rewrite your own first paragraph. Try to engage the reader so that they cannot resist being drawn into your story.

ICT opportunity

Word processors can be a really useful tool to help re-drafting your story. Your teacher may ask you to write a second draft to post on a blog or the school website.

Term 1 Unit 1 Review and assessment

Word builder

1. Read and edit the following notice before it is posted on the school's main noticeboard. There are some errors based on misused homophones hidden in the text. Can you find them all?

> We hope you have herd that the Social Studies Awareness Club is now in operation! We meat every Tuesday afternoon at 2:30 p.m. for one our. It is a little thyme when we paws to think about our country, people, history and rich culture. We plan to do many things, such as field trips to heritage sights, tours and museums. Grab a pear and join us on this adventure. You never no what you will learn!

Let's read

1. Read the extract about the national heroine Nanny of the Maroons and answer the following questions.

> Nanny of the Maroons is the only national heroine in Jamaica. She is remembered for the inspiration she gave to her people in fighting the English Oppressors in the early 18th century. Nanny was a leader of her village, Nanny Town, in the parish of Portland, Jamaica.
>
> According to Beverley Carey's *The Maroon Story*, Nanny died between 1758 –1762. Legend has it that she possessed superhuman powers.
>
> Source: http://www.jnht.com/fast_facts_national_heroes.php

　　1. How many female national heroines are there in Jamaica?

　　2. What did Nanny motivate the people to do?

　　3. When did Nanny wish for people to fight against the English?

　　4. What was the village where Nanny lived?

　　5. According to Jamaican folklore, what was special about Nanny?

 **Grammar builder**

1. Make as many sentences as you can by matching the main clauses on the right with the subordinate clauses on the left. You may begin the sentences with either the main clause or the subordinate clause.

Subordinate clause	Main clause
1 since I was getting home late	Michelle knew dancing was not for her.
2 even when Anthony practised for several months	Shelly knew she wanted to take up dancing.
3 even though the waiting time was long	Sabrina still beat him at chess.
4 after seeing the famous ballerina	We got through quickly.
5 by the end of the first rehearsal	My wife kept my dinner warm in the oven.

2. Make three complex sentences of your own. Remember to use the correct conjunctions and to place the comma in the correct place.

 **Let's write**

Write a letter to someone who remembers what it was like to live before and after Jamaica gained independence. Ask them to give you an account of what it was like to live through those times and about how it has changed.

TERM 1 — Unit 2

Project 7

Speaking and listening

You are going to begin this unit with a focused listening task. You will research some information about Jamaica's landforms.

Discuss

When we listen to a lot of information, it can be difficult to take it all in at once.

Discuss the different techniques that can help you focus while listening. These techniques will improve your chances of recalling the facts and details of what you hear.

Example:

> I stop what I am doing. I stop looking at things around me. I focus on the task by not fidgeting.

> I intentionally clear my mind and stop myself from thinking about, for example, lunch. I always write key words and sometimes draw line drawings.

> When I take notes, I only write the key words. When I read them afterwards, the key words remind me of what I heard.

Focused task

Your teacher will divide you into groups and assign your group one of the topics below to research as a team. Each group member must make brief notes on the topic.

The five topics are:
- Jamaica's varied landforms
- Volcanic origins
- Mountains, plateaus and valleys
- Karst formations
- Wildlife and vegetation

Your teacher will now put you into mixed groups where each member has researched a different topic. Use your notes to report on your topic to the new group. Your new group members should listen attentively and take notes while you present your research.

Plenary

As a whole class, your teacher will ask you for key information on each topic. In your notebooks, create a simple table with the five topics on one side of the table and notes of the points of interest next to each topic on the other side of the table.

Project 7 – An island of contrasts

Word builder

1. Write the definitions for the words below. Then show how these words are used in a sentence.

Word	Definition	Word used in a sentence
magnificent		
beautiful		
fragrant		
generous		
disappointing		
heavy		
distinctive		

2. Choose one of the following techniques to learn the correct spellings for the words in the table above:

- invent mnemonics for the words you cannot spell easily
- identify the number of syllables in each word
- create flashcards so your partner can test you.

ICT opportunity

Use a computer to create a poster with the words. Include a definition of each word and an example of it used in a sentence. There are several features you could explore on a word processor to enhance your poster:

Text effects   Alignment   Highlight   Colour

Term 1 Unit 2

Let's read

1. Read the article on the next page carefully. Take special note of the author's viewpoints.

> **Look and learn**
> The author's viewpoint is how the author feels about the topic. Through their style of writing and word choice, the author's opinion about or attitude towards the subject can be determined.

2. Read the article again. Discuss the purpose of the text. Why do you think the author wrote this article?

3. Identify the words or phrases in the text that indicate whether the author has a positive or negative viewpoint about the landscape in Jamaica.

Jamaica landforms

Travelling around Jamaica is a richly rewarding experience, and not only because of the people you will meet. If you are at all interested in the natural world, then many sights off the beaten track will pique your interest.

Mountain ranges and plateaus

Volcanic in origin, the mountain **ranges** of Jamaica are both interesting and important. The Blue Mountains to the east rise from the coast. As a result, the climb from the base to the **summit** has a remarkably steep **gradient**, as steep as you are likely to find anywhere in the world.

Travel north from the Blue Mountains and you will see the peaks of the John Crow mountains. These are formed from **limestone**, with a different **geology** to the Blue Mountains. The John Crow mountains form a **plateau** of limestone. This type of rock is easily eroded, and so the land develops the distinctive **formations** known as Karst formations. Jamaica has some of the most dramatic Karst landscapes on the planet.

Rivers and waterways

Most of Jamaica's rivers are unnavigable, and so they remain a mysterious and unexplored realm, although those that are able to explore the waterways of the country can be rewarded with some spectacular waterfalls and **intricate** cave systems.

Coasts

Jamaica's coastline is incredibly varied, from the **rugged** northern beaches which are subject to extensive **erosion** to the western beaches of fine sand and luxurious sunsets. In the south, there are some places where 300 foot cliffs drop dramatically into the sea.

All in all, whatever your interest may be, Jamaica has something in its land that lights up your soul.

Term 1 Unit 2

Research and study skills

1. Re-read the article titled *Jamaica landforms*. Make a list of all the words that are in bold.

2. Copy and sort the words on a Venn diagram like the one below. If a word does not belong in either circle, then write it on the outside of the diagram.

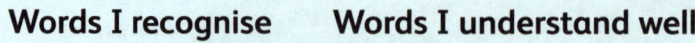
Words I recognise   **Words I understand well**

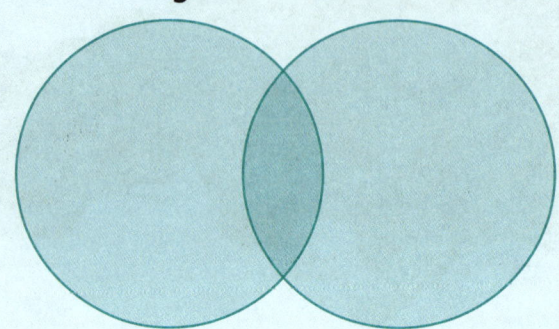

3. If there are words that you recognise but do not understand, find the sentence they are in and try to work out the meaning from the context of the sentence. Once you have thought of possible definitions, you could look up the word in a dictionary or online to see if you were correct.

4. Find some of the locations that are detailed on the Jamaican map in the article and write their compass point locations. For example: *Montego Bay – north west*.

5. Research online or in the library to find out:

    1. Which parts of the island have large populations?
    2. Which parts are almost unpopulated?
    3. Where do most tourists stay?
    4. Is there a relationship between questions 1 and 3 above? Are the areas where tourists stay more populated than other areas in Jamaica?

Project 7 – An island of contrasts

Grammar builder

Remember ⭐☆☆

Adjectives often appear before the noun they describe, but they can also appear after a verb such as *appears*, *seem* or *looks*. They can describe precise details about a noun, but they often also give an indication of the speaker's viewpoint. Try to spot the adjectives in these sentences:

The old carpet looks worn.

Your favourite movie seems scary.

Although it appears angry, that small dog is quite friendly.

1 Look at this sentence. The two adjectives are highlighted in bold. Discuss the different effect of each adjective. Which is more precise and which tells you more about the author's viewpoint? Try substituting different adjectives to change the author's viewpoint.

Travel north from the **magnificent** Blue Mountains and you will reach the **limestone** John Crow mountains.

2 Copy the table that follows and complete it by adding the adjectives below and your own words.

| selfish | loud | scratchy | youthful |
| green | impressive | careful | |

	General	Appearance	Other senses	Personal
Positive viewpoint	magnificent	beautiful	fragrant	generous
Negative viewpoint	disappointing			
Neutral/Factual	distinctive		heavy	

65

3. Compare your table with a partner. Did any of you choose the same adjectives? Can you think of any more together?

Extra challenge

Choose a page at random in a novel, an encyclopaedia or a website that your teacher suggests. Find the adjectives and decide if they are positive, negative or neutral. Compare your results with a partner. Does the type of text chosen affect your results?

Project 7 – An island of contrasts

Let's write

1 Discuss these photographs. Do you know any factual information about them? Discuss what you understand about:
   - how each type of environment is formed
   - where they are found on the island
   - what impact they have on the lives and people of Jamaica.

2 Consider your own personal response to one of these landforms. Think about the following:

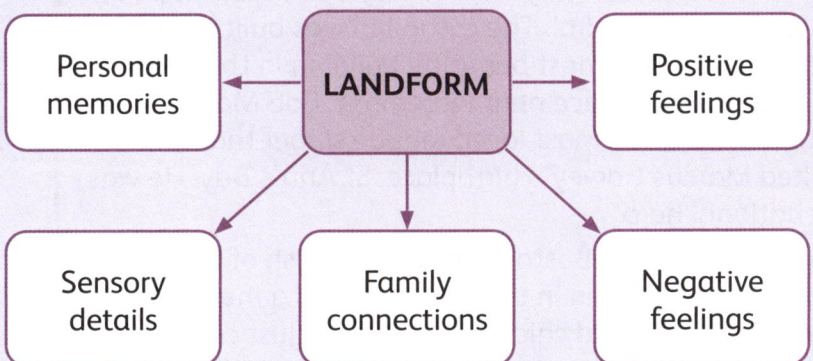

3 Write a paragraph that describes one of the landforms and your experience of it. You should aim to show the reader your viewpoint by the kinds of adjectives you use. For example, do not say "I have a positive viewpoint about this because …". Rather indicate your feelings about the landform by the choice of words you use to describe it. For example: "The mountain slopes glitter as they stand against the majestic bright blue sky."

4 Swap your paragraph with a partner. Can he or she understand your viewpoint from what you have written? Discuss what improvements you both could make.

Project 8

Speaking and listening

> **L👓👓k and learn**
>
> It is important to recognise whether we are being told facts or opinions. If something is mainly factual, we say it is **objective**. If it is mainly an opinion or only about one person, then we say it is **subjective**.

1. Your teacher will read aloud a text about a day trip to Oracabessa. Cover the text while you listen and make a judgement about whether you think it is an objective or subjective text. Report back to the class with your answer.

> We went on a day trip to Oracabessa in St Mary. On the way there we stopped in Spanish Town to visit its amazing cathedral. The cathedral was built in 1552 and is the oldest in Jamaica. It is also the most beautiful building in the country. Then we went to visit Bob Marley's birthplace near Claremont. Bob Marley's music is the best in Jamaica and he is the most loved reggae singer that ever lived. Following this, we visited Marcus Garvey's birthplace, St Ann's Bay. He was Jamaica's most important national hero.
>
> Our next stop was at the coastal village of Boston Bay in the parish of Portland where the jerking of pork and chicken began in the 1960s. This is a method of barbecuing meat which makes the pork and chicken tastier than just cooking with spices in the oven. Finally, we headed back to Kingston via Port Morant in St Thomas.

2. Your teacher will read aloud the text again. Cover the text while you listen.

   1. Form two groups:
      - Group A: listen for **facts** and make notes of key words while you listen.
      - Group B: listen for **opinions** and make notes of key words while you listen.
   2. Come together as a class. Group A reports back to the teacher with their facts. Group B answers with their opinions and explains the reasons for their answers.

Project 8 – Fact or opinion?

> **Remember** ☆ ☆ ☆
>
> Adjectives can be used to indicate a viewpoint. This is one way that writers can disguise their opinions as facts. For example, look at this sentence that a celebrity posted on their social media site:
>
> *This delicious slimming shake makes me feel great!*
>
> Is this sentence written as an opinion or a fact? Look for the adjectives. What facts can you find in the sentence? What opinions are there?

3. As a class, decide whether the text on the previous page was more objective or subjective.

Word builder

Look and learn

Words can form word families. Look at the following family of the word *structure*.

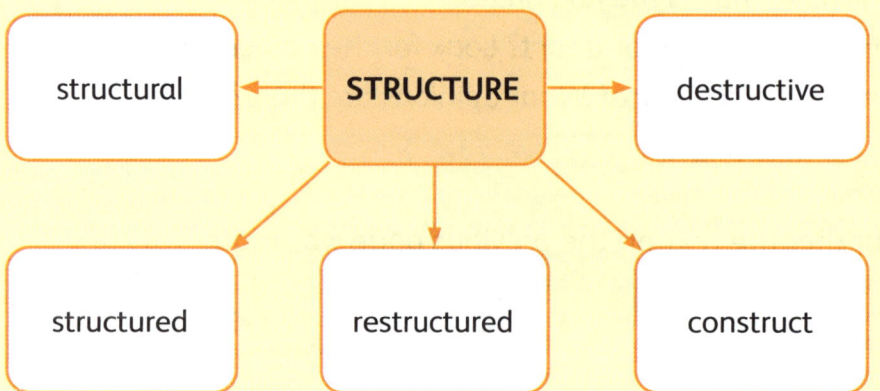

The **root** of the word **structure** is **-struct-**. It means *build*, and from that root, all the other words gain part of their meaning.

1. In pairs, use the words that stem from *-struct-* in sentences to make sure you understand the meanings.

2. Look at these words:
   - atmospheric
   - geology
   - vegetation
   - mountainous
   - volcanic
   - formation

   1. For each word, think of one more word in the word family.

   2. Think of what the root word would be for each word. Draw a table in your notebook like the one below. Use a dictionary or online tool to help you to complete the table with the words above.

Root	Meaning	Related words	Example used in a sentence
struct	builds	structure, destructive	The storm was incredibly destructive.
atmos	air	atmosphere, atmospheric	

Let's read

> **L👀k and learn**
>
> **What is a fact?** A fact refers to something that is true and can be proved to be true. It is **objective**.
>
> **What is an opinion?** An opinion refers to a personal belief. It cannot be proved or disproved. It is **subjective**.

1 The following is a text about trees and other plants in the Jamaican forests. Does it have more facts or opinions? Say why, using examples from the text.

> **Trees and other plants in natural forests**
>
> The forests of Jamaica are full of amazing plants. It's worth going to the forests and mountains just to see the Old Man's Beard hanging from trees and the tree ferns that date back to the time of dinosaurs!
>
> More than 50% of the plants found in the Blue and John Crow Mountains are endemic to Jamaica. This means that these plants are only found naturally in Jamaica.
>
> Some plants, like the Climbing Bamboo (Chusquea altifolia), climb up the trees so that they can reach the sunlight. Other plants, like orchids and bromeliads, live on the branches of the trees. Lichens also grow on the trees and on the rocks in the mountains.

L👀k and learn

What? Any action, movement or event that is taking place.
Where? Details about the location – specific and general.
When? Past, present or future? Once, weekly, ongoing?
Who? Any people, plants or creatures.
Why? What does the text say the reasons are.
How? What explanation is given in the text.

2. The five *Wh-* (and one *How*) question words can be very helpful in lifting information and facts from a text. Find information in the text to go with the question words. Use a visual organiser like the one below to document the information in note form.

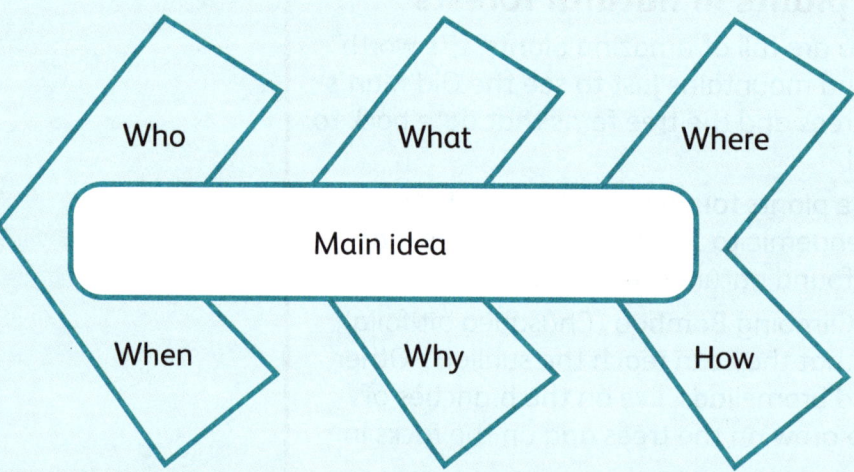

3. What do you think the purpose of this text is? Think about the information and language that the author has used. Why have they chosen to share this with the reader?

Project 8 – Fact or opinion?

Grammar builder

1. Inside the mystery box there is a noun. Read the clues below and see if you can discover the noun.

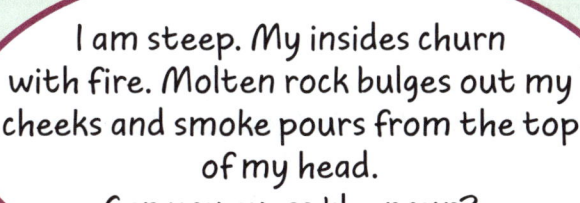

I am steep. My insides churn with fire. Molten rock bulges out my cheeks and smoke pours from the top of my head. Can you guess the noun?

2. Invent some of your own clues for the following nouns: *river, waterfall, pebble, plateau* and *valley*. Consider the clues in the speech bubbles.

You cannot touch or see me, but you can name me. I am as high as you fly, and I am down with you at sea-level. Can you guess the noun?

3. The description above refers to an abstract noun. Which of these words do you think it matches? Justify your reasons.

   mass   measure   altitude   weather   cloud   rain   light

4. Copy the table and add nouns to each column.

Concrete nouns	Abstract nouns
river, waterfall, volcano	altitude, mass, weather

5. Discuss where each of these nouns should be placed in the table above: *oxygen, metre, tragedy, disaster, fire, lake, flood, plateau, mountain.*

73

Let's write

Opinions are like pebbles. They shift and slide.

Facts are like mountains, firm and everlasting beneath our feet.

1. Create a factual presentation about one landform. This should include:
   - accurate technical vocabulary
   - information and scientific facts.

   This short factual paragraph should be written in Standard Jamaican English (SJE).

   Example:
   At least 40% of the higher plants (flowering and non-flowering) are endemic to Jamaica, which means that they are not naturally found anywhere else in the world.

2. Write another paragraph that demonstrates your viewpoint. You should include opinions as well as facts and use adjectives in a way that shows either a positive or a negative slant. This paragraph could be written using Jamaican Creole (JC).

   Example:
   The mountain ranges of Jamaica are both interesting and important.

3. Share your paragraphs with a partner. Help each other with the editing process. Discuss whether your writing meets the criteria in the "Editor's checklist" on the next page.

I noticed that you forgot to …
Can you explain what you mean by …
Let us look up this word in a dictionary.

Project 8 – Fact or opinion?

Editor's checklist

Factual paragraph

- appropriate vocabulary
- accurate factual language
- formal tone
- Standard Jamaican English (SJE)

Opinion paragraph

- adjectives to show viewpoint
- opinions mixed with facts
- informal tone
- Jamaican Creole (JC)

Lk and learn

An important part of the writing process, and also of learning, is **receiving feedback**. A critical friend is someone who you can trust to tell you the truth. Any criticism will be in the form of advice rather than judgement.

4 Read your passages to the class. They will listen and provide feedback once you have finished.

5 While you are listening to other passages from your classmates, use a listening focus chart like the one below to help you notice the use of language and decide how appropriate it is to the task:

Sentence	Standard Jamaican English	Jamaican Creole	Appropriate	Not appropriate	Unsure	Reason

Project 9

Speaking and listening

Valerie Bloom was born in Jamaica and moved to the UK in 1979. Listen to your teacher read the poem *Rain*. Then answer the following questions.

Rain

She makes the trees sway with delight.
She tells the long grass, "Shiver".
She puts the laughter in the stream
And the gurgle in the river.

She drives the thunder grumbling off,
Orders the wind to sing,
Snuffs the lightning's fire out,
Takes the roof tap-dancing

She pours a drink for the thirsty earth,
Washes the face of the sky,
Puts a sparkle on the leaves
And a glint in the ocean's eye

She plays a tattoo on the windowpanes,
Paints doors a darker brown,
And creates a brand-new swimming pool
In the centre of the town

In anger, she will pound the ground
With the force of a cannonball,
But happy, she sings a lullaby,
This celestial waterfall.

by Valerie Bloom

1. Have you heard this poem before? If so, does it seem different this time? Can a poem's meaning change as we get older even though the words stay the same?
2. What poetic features did you hear in the poem?
3. Who is being described in the poem?

Project 9 – Up in the mountains

4 Why is the rain sometimes described as a *cannonball*, but sometimes a *lullaby*?
5 Where are the specific places mentioned?
6 The poet uses a technique called *personification*. Identify how the rain is described as if it is a person. Collect information about whether the poet describes the person's:

- personality
- emotions
- actions
- appearance.

7 What pictures do these techniques paint?
8 Read the poem out loud with your partner pretending that you are the rain. Discuss with your partner what the difference might be if the rain was not personified. Would it have a different effect on you when you read it?

ICT opportunity

- You can listen to the poet being interviewed about being a poet at the *Poetry Archive* website: https://childrens.poetryarchive.org/interviews/an-interview-with-valerie-bloom/
- Remember, you must be sensible when you are online. In pairs, complete the challenge:

  Use a search engine such as Google to search for information on safety rules for children using the internet. Write down three of these rules.

  Compare your answers with the YouTube website by searching for videos titled *Five Internet Safety Tips for Kids*.

Look and learn

In the "ICT opportunity" box, there is a link to a website. Sometimes links get broken (they do not work) because the author or the *search engine* (Google, Bing, Yahoo, etc.) has removed the file or moved it. If this happens, you can still find out information by looking at the link and doing a new search with the key words. For example: *Valerie Bloom interview*.

Extra challenge

Research other poems that use personification. You may have a poetry anthology in class, or your teacher may guide you to a poetry website. Find a collection and copy some for a class display or to keep in a class book of favourite poems.

Word builder

1. The word families in the vocabulary box below demonstrate different examples of spelling rules. Circle which words demonstrate the following rules:
   - Change -*y* to *i* when adding a suffix.
   - Double a consonant.

2. Can you describe the pattern that occurs when adding -*ful* and adding -*fully*? Does this work with other suffixes?

Vocabulary box

big, bigger, biggest
small, smaller, smallest
hope, hopeful, hopefully
beauty, beautiful, beautifully
happy, happily, happiness
disaster, disastrous, disastrously

3. Watch a video clip on homophones. Here is an example video: https://www.bbc.co.uk/education/clips/zsvnp39. Write down the homophones you can hear in your journal.

4. Create a series of flashcards with homophones written on both sides of the card. You can also use paper for this activity. Test your partner by showing them one side of the card. They have to think of the homophone and tell you the spelling that is on the reverse of the card.

Let's read

1. Read the poem titled *The Song of a Blue Mountain Stream* quietly to yourself. Pause to think about the following:

   - What stood out for you?
   - What did you understand?
   - How did you connect with the poem in the following areas: memories, feelings, questions?

> **The Song of the Blue Mountain Stream**
>
> In a cleft remote
> Where white mists float
> Around Blue Mountain's Peak,
> I rise unseen
> Beneath the screen
> Of fog-clouds dank and bleak;
> I trickle, I flow
> To the hills below
> And vales that lie far under,
> From babblings low
> I louder grow
> I shout, I roar, I thunder.
>
> I fall with a rush
> In the morning hush
> While the mountain sleeping lies,
> There swift I sweep,
> Here slow I creep,
> 'Til the sound of my motion dies;
> Oh! I rejoice
> In the night-wind's voice
> As soft it kisses my stream,
> And dance and glimmer
> And glance and shimmer
> Where moon-lit reaches gleam.
>
> With ice-cold wave
> I gently lave
> The flowers as I wander,
> I gloom and glide
> 'Neath Mountain Pride,
> I murmur and meander
> Thru' arched fern dells
> Where fairy-bells
> And violets scent the air
> While calls above
> The soft blue dove
> Its lone voice solitaire.
> And here I crash
> With a silver flash
> Over a mighty crag,
> The echoes ring
> As I headlong fling
> The trees I downward drag;
> 'Til last I pour
> With deafening roar,
> A mountain stream no longer,
> O'er plains below
> And seawards flow
> A river broad and stronger.
>
> by Reginald M. Murray

2. Look for all the references to sound in the poem. What do the nouns, verbs and adjectives used tell you about each sound?

3. Now read the poem aloud to a partner. Does reading the poem aloud give you a new insight? Discuss your responses to Activity 2 together.

4. Read the poem again with your partner, but this time try to make your voice sound like the descriptions in the poem as they change. Does it make a difference to how you understand the poem?

5. Collect information about the following aspects of the poem.
   1. What is it about?
   2. Where is it located?
   3. Who does it speak to?
   4. What is the passage of time like in the poem?
   5. Are there any reasons given for the content of the poem?

6. Think about the language and effects used in this poem.
   1. How is transformation (a change or journey) described in this poem?
   2. How is personification (bringing a non-living thing to life) used in this poem?
   3. How do transformation and personification affect your reponse to the poem?

Extra challenge

Make an artwork that shows the transformation of the Blue Mountain Stream throughout the poem. Include as many details from the poem as possible.

Project 9 – Up in the mountains

Grammar builder

> **Look and learn**
> **Adjectives** are used to modify nouns. They tell us more specific information about a noun.
> **Adverbs** are used to modify verbs. They describe the verb more fully.

1. Adverbs can also be used to modify adjectives. Look at the following sentences:

   - The cold water flowed over my toes.
   - The refreshingly cold water flowed soothingly over my toes.

   1. Underline the adjective and the verb in the first sentence.
   2. Circle the adverbs that modify the adjective and verb in the second sentence.

2. Compare the sentences and describe the effect of the words *refreshingly* and *soothingly*.

3. Look at the following adverbs that can also be used to modify adjectives. Then underline the adjectives and complete the sentences with an appropriate adverb. Use a different adverb for each sentence.

   Vocabulary box

   very   quite   extremely   barely

   1. The ice cream was _____ cold and gave me a headache.
   2. The music was _____ loud.
   3. The tea was _____ warm enough to drink.
   4. The test was _____ easy, so I am sure I have passed.

4. Write a sentence in your notebook for each adverb, showing how it can modify an adjective. Use the examples above and the second sentence from Activity 1 as a guide.

Let's write

1. Imagine you are an earthquake, a volcano or a tsunami. Consider your five senses as you advance on the landforms in your path. What is your aim? Where are you going? How will you get there? What are you doing?

2. Brainstorm the following areas and make notes on how your senses are being used:

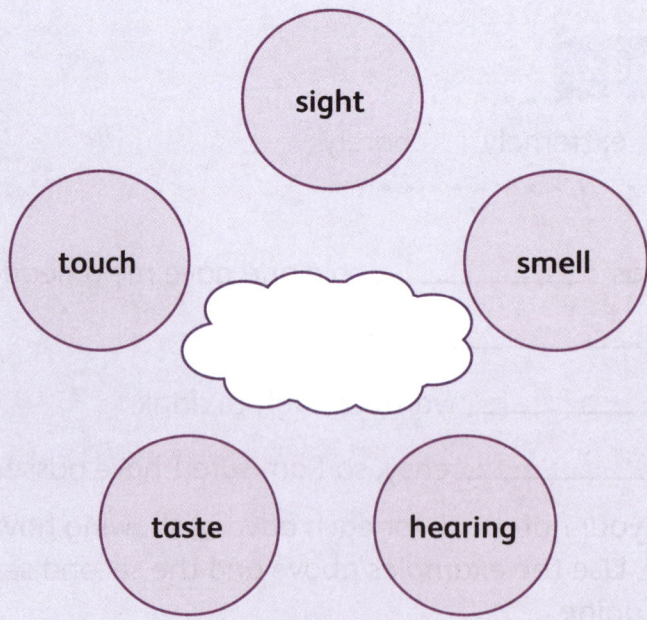

3 Now think about your emotions and answer the questions that follow.

   1 What would you like to accomplish?

   2 What challenges lie in your way?

   3 What emotions drive you on your quest?

   4 How do you feel about the victims of your destruction?

4 Write a diary entry describing your experiences using personification and figurative language. Record three days: the build-up, the event and the aftermath.

Day 1	Day 2	Day 3
Describe your emotions and the purpose that drives you on. Describe with anticipation and feeling.	Give a sensory account of the big event. Imagine yourself as a giant person, ripping, tearing, crunching, and include details of all the senses.	This could be a moment of quiet reflection, with a sense of the thoughts and feelings that remain after the excitement is over.

Editor's checklist

- adverbs and adjectives
- sensory description
- appropriate use of Standard Jamaican English (SJE) or Jamaican Creole (JC)

5 Swap your work with your partner. Give each other feedback on what is done well and what can be improved.

Project 10

Speaking and listening

1. Stories are usually told in words, sentences and paragraphs, but we can also use proverbs such as *A picture says a thousand words*.

   1. In small groups, discuss this proverb and decide if you agree.

   2. With your group, discuss any sayings or proverbs and their meanings your group members know. They are often meant to be wise or to explain something important.

      For example: *Talk and taste your tongue.* = *Think before you speak.*

   3. Are the proverbs you know usually spoken in Standard Jamaican English (SJE) or Jamaican Creole (JC)? What do your group members think?

Project 10 – Pictures that tell stories

2. In pairs, study the photographs and discuss what you understand from the pictures. Organise your observations into two categories:
   - Facts we are certain about
   - Possibilities and opinions

3. With your partner, think of a series of questions you can ask about each picture to find out more details for certain. Use these words: *What*, *Who*, *When*, *Where*, *Why* and *How*.

4. Join another pair of students and pool your questions together. Choose the best three to share with the class.

Term 1 Unit 2

Word builder

Remember ☆☆☆

Homonyms are words which are spelled the same but have different meanings.
Antonyms are words which are opposite in meaning.
Synonyms are words which have the same (or very similar) meaning.

Vocabulary box

| disaster | destruction | emergency | community | casualty |
| victim | flood | tragedy | relief | |

1 Read the words from the vocabulary box to your partner. Discuss whether there are any pairs that are synonyms. Do any of the words have more than one meaning? Make a list of the words that are homonyms and their different meanings. Can you think of a synonym for any of the words?

2 Look at the photographs in the "Speaking and listening" lesson again. Think of nouns, adjectives or verbs that describe one or more of the photographs and write them in a table like the one below.

Nouns	Adjectives	Verbs

3 Find synonyms in a thesaurus for each word that you wrote on your list in Activity 1 above. Add these to your list.

Extra challenge

Write a short paragraph using the synonyms to describe a scene in one of the photographs.

ICT opportunity

Look up an online dictionary. You will see that for each word they will give an alternative definition (homonym) and often show the synonyms as well as antonyms for each meaning.

Project 10 – Pictures that tell stories

Let's read

1 Read the text and decide whether the following sentences are true or false.

> Most agree the prime time to have a holiday in Jamaica is during the start of "winter", November to mid-December, with temperatures averaging 80°F, even though the most popular season begins mid-December and ends mid-April. Therefore, the crowds are plentiful during this period. Summer, June to August, sees temperatures soar to above 90°F in some places, so it is much warmer and brings a slight increase in rainfall.

1 The best time to holiday in Jamaica is throughout winter.

2 Temperatures reach their average of 80°F after two weeks into December.

3 The most popular season lasts for five months.

4 During June to August, temperatures reach 90°F throughout Jamaica.

5 There is less rain in the winter.

2 Correct all the false sentences in your notebook.

Research and study skills

Graphs are drawings that show information called **data**. Data can be presented as lines, shapes or pictures.

Look and learn

A **vertical** line rises straight up from the bottom to the top. A **horizontal** line is from left to right.

A graph has two axes, *x* and *y*. The *x*-axis is horizontal and the *y*-axis is vertical.

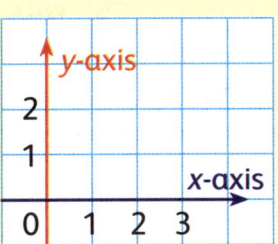

In pairs, analyse and become familiar with the two graphs on the next page. Look at the axes and the data that is being measured.

87

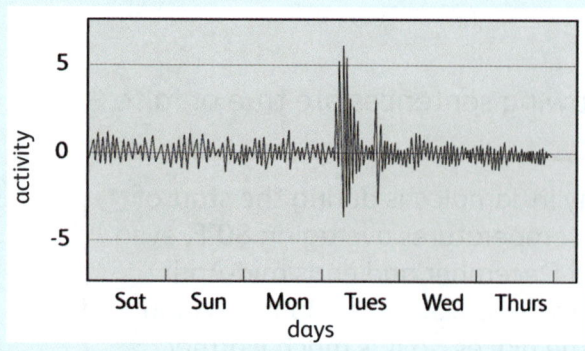
A seismograph showing activity before and after an earthquake.

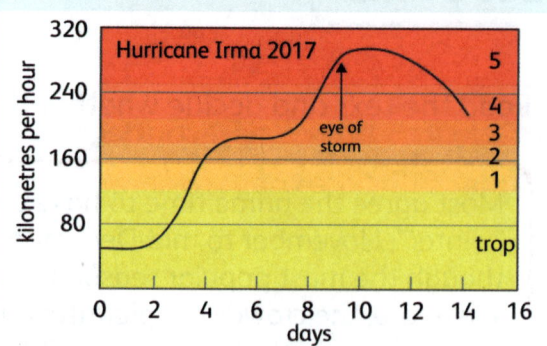
A line graph showing the windspeed during a hurricane.

Extracting information

- What is the same and what is different about the two graphs?
- What features has the author used to enable these graphs to be understood?
- Use words to describe the figures of each line graph.
- Describe where you can detect these phenomena in each graph:
    - Aftershocks
    - The eye of the storm
    - Warning signs

Making predictions

In pairs, make hypotheses or judgements based on your knowledge of the weather. Draw a graph with an *x*-axis and *y*-axis to display data. Predict when the next hurricane or strong winds may occur and plot the temperatures and rainfall data on your graph over a twelve-month period. Research temperature and rainfall graphs online to guide you.

Project 10 – Pictures that tell stories

Grammar builder

Look and learn

Sentences, clauses and connectors

Conjunctions are connecting words. Common conjunctions include *and, so, or, but, while, when, where*.

Conjunctions can be used to join two parts of a sentence, two nouns or two verbs.

Sentences: <u>Montego Bay is on the north coast</u> **while** <u>Kingston is in the south east.</u>

Nouns: <u>I would like a mango</u> **and** <u>a banana.</u>

Verbs: <u>Everyone was singing</u> **and** <u>dancing at the carnival.</u>

Simple, compound and complex sentences

- A simple sentence = a **subject** and one **verb**:

  The hurricane swept into the mainland.

- A compound sentence = [a main clause] + a connective + [a main clause]:

  [Jamaica has warm weather in the winter.] [Jamaica has hot weather in the summer.]

  Jamaica has warm weather in the winter, **but** *it has hot weather in the summer.*

- A complex sentence = [a main clause] + [a connective that comes before the subordinate clause]:

  The earthquake was strong, yet there was no damage.

1 Conjunctions have different meanings. Match the functions 1-7 with each group (a-g). If there are any conjunctions or words you are not sure about, use a dictionary or an online tool to look up the meanings.

1 an alternative

2 express the result of something

3 to add information

4 the reason for something

5 to contrast information

6 to sequence points

7 if not

89

a Firstly, next, finally _____

b and, in addition _____

c but, however _____

d because _____

e or _____

f so _____

g unless _____

2 Complete the sentences. Use *and*, *but*, *so*, *unless*.

1 The team of relief workers was exhausted, _____ they continued work.

2 The earthquake shook the rocks violently, _____ the buildings came crashing down.

3 Many volunteers supported the emergency teams, _____ they needed all the help they could get.

4 Food supplies will run out, _____ they send more supplies.

3 In pairs, write your own sentences using the following linking phrases:

- In order to …
- As a result of …
- As a consequence of …
- The effect of which is …

Project 10 – Pictures that tell stories

Let's write

You are going to create a presentation for your class about a problem in your community, such as:

- the erosion of hillsides
- deforestation
- unsafe paths
- the effects of industry or tourism.

Your presentation should have three stages:

1. What is the problem?
2. Why is it important?
3. What should be done and why?

Planning stage 1

To state the problem, you will need to compare and contrast. For example:

- More people are killed each year by falling buildings during earthquakes than from drowning in ponds.
- People care more about having a job than about the effects of industry on the environment.

Find information about your topic and your problem. Look for sources you can use that will give you objective information.

Adjective	Comparative	Superlative
steep	steeper	steepest
strong	stronger	strongest
dangerous	more dangerous	most dangerous

Remember ☆☆☆

Include the above adjectives to compare and contrast different aspects in your presentation. Support your presentation with a visual, such as a graph or a diagram to illustrate the problem.

ICT opportunity

You could create slides to support your presentation. It is important that the slides and images enhance your talk and make your meaning clearer. It is not effective to use the slides to display your text.

Planning stage 2

This planning stage should discuss the causes and effects of the issue. For this, you can use conjunctions or linking words to show the causal relationship.

Cause and effect, for example: *Farmers remove vegetation on hillsides **in order to** use it as farmlands which leads to soil erosion.*

Remember

Use linking phrases to show the effect of the problem. For example: *As a result of, As a consequence of, The effect of which is, because, therefore, so that, such that.*

Planning stage 3

In this planning stage, you should restate the problem along with potential solutions. Include a diagram that will benefit your presentation and also show how the solution works.

Problem and solution, for example: *Teaching farmers terracing helps to reduce soil erosion **while** still making use of the land resource.*

Editor's checklist

- accurate technical vocabulary
- use of conjunctions and linking phrases for clear explanations
- visuals support that does not replace the speech

Feedback

While you listen to one another's presentations, consider these questions:

- Did the visuals enhance the presentation?
- Was the message stronger because of the use of the visuals or was it weakened?
- Was the use of language appropriate to the task?

Decide as a class which presentation was the most convincing and why.

Project 11

Speaking and listening

1. Use *Wh-* questions in response to information. Here are some scenarios:
   - What if there were an earthquake off the coast of Kingston?
   - What if a hurricane tore through a nearby island?
   - What happens when a volcano erupts?
   - What happens when hillsides and mountainous regions are deforested?

> **L👀k and learn**
> A possible idea or situation rather than an actual one is called **hypothetical**.

2. Formulate a response to one of these scenarios. Think about a chain of events and the important questions:

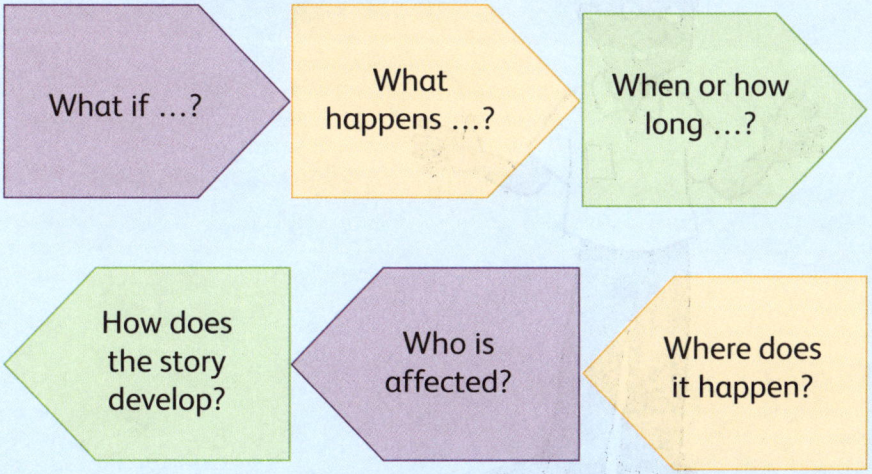

3. Listen to a partner's responses and make notes about the use of language, using a table like the one below. Suggest changes that your partner might want to make before they share their responses with the rest of the class.

Sentence	Standard Jamaican English (SJE)	Jamaican Creole (JC)	Appropriate	Not appropriate	Unsure	Reason

4. Share the responses as a class. Be ready to ask further questions at the end. You can use phrases like:
   - When you said …, did you mean …?
   - Can you give me further information about …?
   - Are you saying that … or …?

Remember ☆☆☆

Always remember to ask questions politely – even if you disagree. The point of discussion is to understand each other's point of view better, not to defeat someone in an argument.

Word builder

1. In pairs take turns to read aloud this passage.

   Tsunamis can have catastrophic effects. Some have a short duration and are caused by earthquakes and volcanic eruptions, yet their impact is often intense and the following destruction can last for decades. Other disasters can be steady in their progress, yet their effects are no less devastating. For example, according to scientists the issues of climate change are affecting weather-systems and ocean currents. This is having an impact on the flora and fauna of coastal habitats and in turn affects the livelihoods of people all over the world.

2. Read aloud the words below and identify the number of syllables in each word.

   tsunami _____   effects _____

   duration _____   eruption _____

   impact _____   decade _____

   progress _____   devastating _____

   climate _____   flora _____

   fauna _____   livelihood _____

3. With your partner discuss the words in Activity 2. Which ones are unfamiliar? Use a dictionary or online tool to look up the meaning of those words and to check the number of syllables in any words you may find difficult to pronounce.

4. With your partner, write a short passage about a disaster caused by a tsunami. Include as many words as you can from the words in Activity 3.

5. Compare your passage with other pairs of students in the class. Ask your teacher to announce which pair included the most words in their passage.

Let's read

1. Below is an extract from a blog titled *What if …?* Use evidence from the text to explain why you think this is an appropriate title.

> **What if …?**
>
> What if the sea were to recede rapidly from the coastal regions? This is what happens if a tsunami is forming in the ocean. It might seem unlikely, but often the first warning sign of a tsunami is the water being pulled back out into the ocean. Incredibly, knowing this fact saved a few people from the devastating effects of a tsunami in the Indian Ocean in 2004.
>
> Tsunamis are generated when a geological event, such as an earthquake or a volcanic eruption, happens under the sea. In certain conditions, these can cause a portion of the sea floor to move. This then generates strong forces in the motion of the water.
>
> Were this to occur off the Jamaican coast, the situation could be severe. A tsunami is sometimes called a *tidal wave*. The reality is different from how it is shown in movies; however, the effects are no less devastating. The waters appear to rise like an incredibly high tide, though unlike a tide, they just keep rising and rising.
>
> Coastal towns and low-lying areas would be the worst affected. Those that were able to flee to higher ground would return to a scene of utter destruction, unlike anything recorded in Jamaican history.
>
> Having said all this – it is highly unlikely that such an event would occur, and I think we have more pressing issues to concern ourselves with.

2. Describe what you may notice as a first warning of a tsunami.

3. The author writes that the first sign of a tsunami "might seem unlikely". Explain this, using evidence from the text.

4. Summarise the causes of a tsunami.

5. Find and copy a phrase that suggests that the author is not especially worried about it ever happening.

6. Explain in your own words how a tsunami could affect your life, or the lives of your family and friends. Think about the long-term effects and not just the immediate impact, and why you think these things would happen.

Project 11 – What if there is a tsunami?

Grammar builder

Look and learn

Demonstrative pronouns and **adjectives** modify nouns, the most popular are *this*, *that*, *these* and *those*:

- *This/These* refers to something near to the speaker in space or time: *I brought **this/these** from the shop.*
- *That/Those* refers to something that is more distant: *Pass me **that** book/**those** books please.*

Demonstrative adjectives are followed by nouns: **That** <u>chicken curry</u> smells delicious.

Demonstrative pronouns replace the noun or noun phrase: *I watched <u>the movie Titanic</u> again.* **That** *movie is the best.*

Remember ☆☆☆

A **pronoun** is a word that is used to replace a noun. Look at the table below.

First person	Second person	Third person
I	you	he/she/it
we	yours	they
me		his/hers
mine		theirs
ours		them

1. Identify whether the pronouns are singular or plural by writing "S" or "P" next to the pronouns in the table. Can you identify the possessive pronouns and the personal pronouns in the table above? Underline the possessive pronouns.

2. Look and discuss the following table. Demonstrative pronouns are used in the following ways:

As a pronoun – to replace a noun	As an adjective – to point to a noun
Where is that?	Where is that book?
Please leave those alone.	Please leave those biscuits alone.
Did you bring these?	Did you bring these presents?

97

Term 1 Unit 2

1. Look for these pronouns in the text titled *What if ...?* on page 96. Identify whether they are used as pronouns or adjectives.

2. Write a sentence using each word as a pronoun and as an adjective.

Extra challenge

Pronouns such as these in Standard Jamaican English (SJE) are spelled and pronounced differently to those in Jamaican Creole (JC). Create a passage using them in Jamaican Creole (JC) and then swap your passage with your partner. Convert your partner's into Standard Jamaican English (SJE).

Project 11 – What if there is a tsunami?

Let's write

1 Look at the storyboard below. Complete the sentences to tell the story.

Firstly, I noticed …

Following that, …

Only then did I …

Just when I thought it was all over, …

After what seemed like forever, …	From that moment on, …

2 Use the storyboard technique to tell your own *What if …?* story. Choose from the following options:

> These sequencing phrases help the reader follow the pattern and structure of the story.

Option A – Turn the storyboard from this lesson into a full story of six paragraphs.
Option B – Create your own story board for a different *What if …?* story.

Planning

- Create your storyboard.
- Include a topic sentence for each frame.
- Brainstorm sensory detail for each frame. Note adjectives, nouns and verbs to describe the five senses and the thoughts and emotions relevant to each stage.

Writing

Use the six topic sentences to structure your story. Once the topic sentences are in place, the sensory notes will help you fill out the details of each paragraph. Finish each paragraph with a description of the thoughts and emotions as the events unfold.

Feedback

When your storyboard is complete, exchange it with a partner. Read each other's stories and check carefully for:

- accurate punctuation
- accurate tenses
- effective use of sensory details.

Give your partner helpful feedback on how to improve their story.

L👀k and learn
A common mistake when writing stories is for the verb tenses to change throughout. Look carefully to see whether your partner has begun writing in past tenses and then switched to present tenses somewhere in the story.

Re-drafting

Listen carefully to your partner's advice. You may not agree, but listen openly and be prepared to make changes where necessary.

Project 12

Speaking and listening

Role play what it would be like to be a news team arriving at the scene to report on the aftermath of a disaster. You could choose the following roles:

- newsreader in the studio
- roving reporter at the scene
- witnesses to be interviewed
- expert interviewed in the studio.

1. As a group, decide on the type of disaster your group will role play. This may depend on your knowledge or the area you think will be most interesting to cover. This is a task where everyone will contribute, so you will need to take everyone's point of view into consideration, before making a shared decision.

Remember ☆☆☆

When you have to make group decisions, it is important that everyone has a chance to have their voice heard and to come to a consensus. You may not personally agree with someone's viewpoint, but you need to respect the ideas of everyone.

2. You will need to make the following decisions:
    - Who will speak in Standard Jamaican English (SJE) and who will use Jamaican Creole (JC)? Can you justify these decisions?
    - Will you use facts or opinions in your role play? Will this be different for different characters?

- What different parts of speech and grammatical techniques will each role require? Who will use adjectives and adverbs? Who will use complex sentences?
- Work as a group to brainstorm some ideas for the different roles:

Role	Standard Jamaican English (SJE) or Jamaican Creole (JC)	Language structures	Vocabulary
Newsreader			
Roving reporter			
Witness			
Expert			

3. Work as a group and prepare the questions below together. Discuss the different types of questions that are likely to be used and the kinds of responses to expect.
   - What questions will the interviewer ask the witnesses?
   - What questions will the interviewer ask the expert?
4. Rehearse and perform the scenes. You may want to create cue cards to help remember the main points of a speech.

L👀k and learn
Creating cue cards is much the same as writing notes. You only need to write down the key words – just enough to jog your memory.

ICT opportunity

Listen to a news report or part of a documentary that reports the aftermath of a natural disaster. Create a digital presentation that covers the following areas:
- causes
- effect on the environment
- consequences for humans.

Word builder

1. Read the words from the vocabulary box and identify the number of syllables in each word.

2. With your partner, discuss which meanings are familiar and circle the words you are unsure about. Use a dictionary or online tool to look up the meaning of the words you do not know.

Vocabulary box

obliterated	receded	possessions	devastating
unstable	submerged	queues	rubble
makeshift	national	peril	ongoing

3. With your partner, select three words and write a sentence for each showing its meaning.

4. Join another pair of students and compare your sentences.

5. Sort the words into the following groups. Identify any difficult vocabulary words where you may make mistakes in spelling them.

Has a prefix:	Has a suffix:	Has an unusual spelling pattern:
Contains double letters:	Has a common homonym:	Unfamiliar to me:

6. Add these words to your spelling journal. Select five words and highlight a good strategy for remembering the spelling: choose from mnemonics, breaking into syllables, learning the prefix and root, and visual strategy.

Extension task

Look through this unit. Find the technical words from each lesson and add them to your spelling journal. Sort them into groups depending on spelling patterns.

ICT opportunity

Create a class blog with all the spellings from the term. Your teacher could post it on the school website so that you can refer to it again, later in the year.

The blog could include quotations from people in the class, with advice about how to spell different words.

Let's read

1
1. This is an extract from a news report. Using only the picture, predict what the report is about. Suggest some details that the report might include.

2. Read the news report carefully. How was your prediction correct? How was it incorrect?

It has been called a national disaster. In fact, it may be the worst national emergency in living memory. People are only now, more than ten days since the waters rose, burst the banks and submerged everything in its path, returning to their homes. However, for most, there is little to return to.

It was only once the waters receded that the extent of the damage became fully apparent. People have returned to find their homes obliterated, buildings unstable and possessions caked in mud. Precious family heirlooms, documents, electronics, pets – all lie buried beneath rubble and many will never be found.

While the loss of possessions may be disheartening, it is the human story that is truly devastating. The worst is not over. The ongoing peril that families, grandparents, children and adults find themselves struggling against will continue for many, many months and years. Many families are living in makeshift shelters, in very few places is there clean running water and the queues for emergency supplies snakes down the streets, where once the happy children played.

2
1. Choose an appropriate headline for this news report.

2. Summarise this article in no more than two sentences. The aim is for someone to have a good understanding of the article by only reading your sentences.

3. Swap your sentences with your partner's. Whose do you think summarises the information best?

3 How would you describe the author's viewpoint?

Research and study skills

L👀k and learn

Fact and opinion are often woven together in texts and speeches, so it is important to understand the difference. This can help you with your research and study skills. You will develop critical and analytical skills. This means you learn to compare and contrast, explain why things happen and evaluate ideas and form opinions in reading and listening.

Phrases used to describe objective facts:

- The report **confirms** …
- Scientists have **discovered** …
- **According to** the results of the survey …
- The investigation **demonstrated** …

Phrases used to describe subjective opinions:

- The author **claimed** that …
- The report **suggests** that …
- Her **view** is that …
- Scientists **predict** that …

1. Read the text in the "Let's read" lesson and underline all the facts with a straight line and the opinions with a wavy line.

2. Copy the table below in your notebook and enter the facts and opinions you identified in Activity 1.

Facts	Opinions

3. Make a judgement about the text's objectivity or subjectivity. Share your reasons with your classmates.

Project 12 – The aftermath

Grammar builder

1. This is a review of the four main grammar areas you have learned in this unit. Work with a partner or in a group to discuss each.

Abstract and concrete nouns
- How many different abstract and concrete nouns can you list about the topic of landforms and natural disasters?

Demonstrative pronouns
- Create a poster with symbols that demonstrate the meaning of a range of demonstrative pronouns and demonstrative adjectives.

Linking phrases and conjunctions
- Write sentences on pieces of paper, then mix and match.
- Decide on the most appropriate conjunction or linking phrase to join the pairs of sentences.

Adjectives and adverbs
- Select a random page of a reading text. List any adverbs that are used and decide whether they are modifying a verb or an adjective.

2. Look at the four boxes again with your teacher. Share with the class the responses and examples that you came up with in your group.

Extension task
Write a short paragraph or just one sentence that demonstrates all of the grammar skills from this unit. Enquire whether there is an opportunity to publish examples of the learning from your class this term on the school website.

Self-check
- How confident are you about using each of the grammar skills?
- List the skills and draw the emoji that matches how you feel about each skill.

Grammar	☹	OK	👍
Abstract nouns			
Asking questions			
Linking phrases			
Main and subordinate clauses			

Term 1 Unit 2

Let's write

Apply personification to a landform such as a cliff, a river, etc. Write a persuasive letter to the landform. The point of the letter is to convince the landform to protect your community from an impending natural disaster. This is your chance to improve all the writing skills you learned this term.

> **Editor's checklist**
> Your letter should include:
> - technical vocabulary
> - accurate punctuation
> - organisation of ideas in paragraphs
> - complex sentences
> - formal Standard Jamaican English (SJE).

To plan your writing, follow these prompts:
- Choose a natural disaster that may threaten your community.
- Using your knowledge of landforms, choose one that may be able to protect the community.
- Decide on how to show your respect to the landform.
- Choose some phrases that demonstrate the urgency of the situation.

This paragraph planner may help, including some suggested topic sentences.

Project 12 – The aftermath

	Address
Dear Mr Cliff,	
I am writing in the most important of circumstances.	
The first reason I would urge you to consider is …	
In addition, you will surely see that …	
Unless you agree to support our cause, …	
Yours sincerely, …	

With your partner, edit your letters where necessary whilst you work through the "Editor's checklist" on the previous page.

109

Term 1 Unit 2 Review and assessment

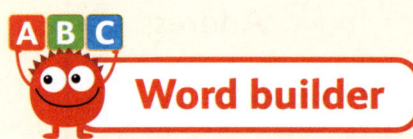

Word builder

1 Write sentences to show how the meaning of a word is changed by adding the suffixes -*ful* and -*less*.

Root	Suffix	Used in a sentence
care	-ful	
harm	-less	
fear		
hope		
use		

Let's read

1 Read the poem several times, each time making notes about the ideas that come to you.

2 What is the poem about, children or people at church? Which words in the poem help you to come to this conclusion?

3 How does the poet feel about the subject of the poem? Quote one line from each stanza which supports your view.

4 What do you think *I can hear the gospel/ Of little feet* means? What does it help you to understand about the children?

Children coming from school

I can hear the gospel
Of little feet
Go choiring
Down the dusty asphalt street.
Beneath the vast
Cathedral of sky
With the sun for steeple
Evangeling with laughter
Go the shining ones
The little people.

by Roger Mais

Review and assessment

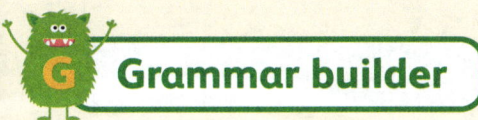 **Grammar builder**

Like any other pronoun, demonstrative pronouns replace nouns in sentences. The noun phrase in the example can be replaced by the demonstrative pronoun *that*.

The outfit you are wearing looks lovely. **That** looks lovely.

Demonstrative adjectives behave like every other adjective; they tell you more about the noun or its replacement. The demonstrative adjective in the example tells you which class is being spoken about.

That class did a brilliant job!

1. Read the sentences, then decide whether the underlined word is a demonstrative pronoun or a demonstrative adjective. Provide a reason for your choice. Then decide whether you would make a different choice given the alternative condition.

Sentences	DP*	DA**	Reason	Alternative condition	Same choice?
1 Those pastries in the shop showcase are my mother's favourite.				Delete the phrase *pastries in the shop showcase*.	
2 This book should be returned to the library immediately.					
3 This really hurts my back.				Insert exercise sequence after the word *This*.	
4 That hat is perfect for silly hat day!				Replace *hat* with the word *sombrero*.	
5 These are so tasty, they must be bad for you.					

DP* – Demonstrative pronoun; DA** – Demonstrative adjective

 **Let's write**

Imagine that you are a reporter working for a well-known newspaper in Jamaica. Your assignment, as the hurricane season approaches, is to write a report about how attitudes to hurricanes and hurricane preparations have changed or remained the same over the last 30 years.

This is a piece which requires the use of comparing and contrasting. Ensure that you make a list of the relevant words as you are planning your report. You may need to think about what people's attitudes to hurricanes were in the past compared to now.

TERM 2

Unit 1

Project 13

Speaking and listening

This lesson is about light and sound. To begin, let's find out what we already know, or think we know, about light.

1 In groups, decide on which rules you think should be agreed on and followed regarding communication in the classroom. Discuss these questions:

   1 How will you make sure that no one is interrupted while speaking or ignored?

   2 What should you do when someone is asking a question?

   3 How will you deal with disagreements or if someone feels they are not being listened to?

   ICT opportunity

   Use a publishing or design app to create a poster showing your communication rules. This will be useful in many other lessons as well.

2 Work in groups. Discuss the topic of light and how it is relevant in each of the photographs below. Choose one group member to scribe (write) the group's ideas on a large sheet using the following mind map. Remember to record all the ideas, even if you think they are not true.

Project 13 – Light in our lives

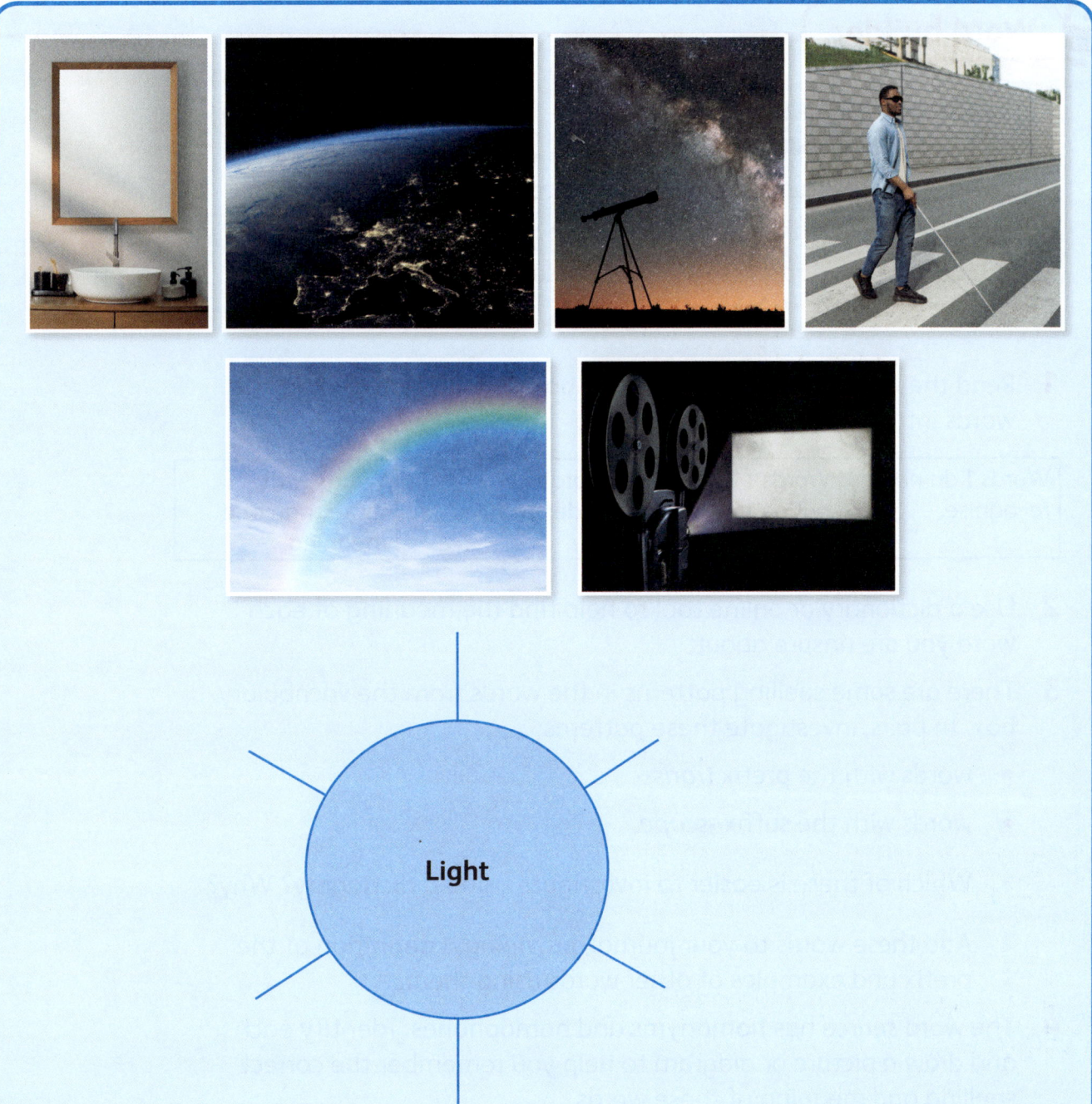

3 Share your group's findings with the class. Your scribe can tell the class what is on your sheet.

4 Discuss which of the findings are *facts* and which are possibly untrue or could be *opinions*. Are there any ways to tell whether something is an opinion?

Word builder

Vocabulary box

lightning	translucent	vibrate	microscope
reflection	transparent	prism	source
refraction	opaque	telescope	colourful

1 Read the words from the vocabulary box to your partner. Sort the words into the following categories:

Words I do not recognise.	Words I recognise but do not understand.	Words I understand.	Words with more than one meaning.

2 Use a dictionary or online tool to help find the meaning of each word you are unsure about.

3 There are some spelling patterns in the words from the vocabulary box. In pairs, investigate these patterns:

- words with the prefix *trans-*
- words with the suffix *-scope*.

  1 Which of these is easier to investigate using a dictionary? Why?

  2 Add these words to your journal, providing a definition of the prefix and examples of other words using them.

4 The word *source* has homonyms and homophones. Identify each and draw a picture or diagram to help you remember the correct spelling and meaning of these words.

5 Can you think of homonyms for the word *light*?

6 Can you spot the errors in the text below? Correct them and write the correct sentences in your journal.

> The lightening storm was fierce.
> You can use a microwave for looking at small objects, and a telescope for observing lite from far away.
> An opauqe object may be very coulorfull.

114

Project 13 – Light in our lives

Extra challenge

Aim to become familiar with technical vocabulary and be able to sight read the words as well as notice common spelling errors as we will be using technical vocabulary throughout this topic. Try to develop a fun test for your partner or the class. You could create anagrams or a word search, or think of another fun idea.

Let's read

1. Skim this text for about one minute. Then, in pairs, decide which school textbook you would expect to see a text like this in and why.

Suddenly the light dawned on me

This is what Einstein should have said when he first realised an astonishing fact about the Universe: nothing can travel faster than the speed of light. It is as if the Universe has a speed limit, albeit a very generous limit. Scientists have measured the speed of light as 300 million metres per second. Even at that speed, the distances of space are so large that it takes eight minutes for the light from the Sun to reach our planet. Light from the nearest galaxy takes years, even hundreds or thousands of years to reach us.

You will have noticed the speed of light yourself. Think of a thunderstorm. When the sky is lit up by lightning, we often have to wait for a count of 10, 20 or even 30 seconds before the rolling sound of thunder reaches us. In fact, some people use this to calculate the distance of the storm. We know that sound is sluggish in comparison – a mere 300 metres per second, approximately. We can use the difference in time it takes the sound and light from a storm to reach us, to calculate the distance.

The way sound and light travel is very different. Although they both travel as waves, sound requires a medium – something to travel through – such as air or water. This in part accounts for the difference in speed between the two. However, you will also have noticed that even light has to slow down sometimes. When you see light refracted in water, this is where the light waves are slowed by the water itself, just like when you try to run through the shallows back to shore.

2. The text contains facts as well as opinions. Complete the table below by scanning the text to find any appropriate information.

	Fact	Opinion	Unsure
Sound travels at 300 metres per second.			
Einstein's discovery is astonishing.			
Light travels at a constant speed.			
Light travels as a wave.			

3 Find these words in the text. Explain their meaning in the context of the sentences in the text:

| sluggish   generous   mere   medium   accounts |

Extra challenge

In your notebook, write other synonyms or phrases to replace the words in Activity 3.

Research and study skills

1 As a class, share all the facts and opinions you have collected from your "Let's read" lesson and discussions on the theme of *Light in our lives*. Create a mind map together, using the following headings.

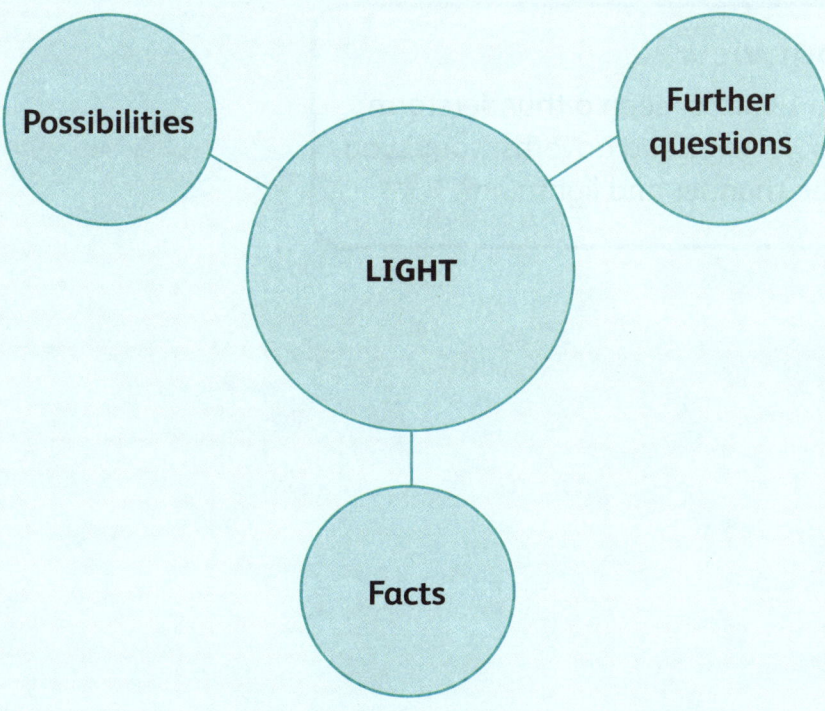

2 Use skimming and scanning to research further information and facts about the properties of light. Look for scientific texts in your class or ask your teacher whether you could search online. Make notes and share them with your class. You could display the facts in a graphic organiser for everyone in the class to use.

3 You will prepare three paragraphs for your journal in your "Let's write" lesson. Each paragraph will cover one of the headings from the visual organiser you created in Activity 1. Create a reference list. This is a list of the books and other sources of information you have used to gather your information.

- Here is an example of how to create a reference for a book: author, title, page references.

  For example: A Smith, Learn About Light, p30-32

- For more precise referencing, you can also include the publisher.

4 Compare your list of references with a partner. Sort your references into two groups: those which you think will be mostly objective facts and those which might also contain opinions.

> **What's your view?**
> Have you ever heard or seen a thunderstorm? What verbs, adjectives and adverbs would you use to describe thunder and lightning?

Project 13 – Light in our lives

Grammar builder

Remember ☆☆☆

Scientific writing often uses present tenses. Can you spot which of the sentences below use present tenses?

- *Isaac Newton discovered how to split light.*
- *When you use a telescope, it focuses light using a lens.*
- *We are going to perform an experiment.*

L👀k and learn

Modal auxiliaries are verbs used to express ability, opportunity, a request, to give permission, and to show possibility or impossibility. To express ability the modal verb *can* is used for the present and changes to *could* for the past.

Present: *The lit candle **can** produce light.*

Past: *The torch **could** produce light, but now the battery is dead.*

1 Have a look at the photographs. Copy and complete the table below for each image.

It **can** produce its own light.	It **cannot** produce its own light.	It **could** produce its own light before but **cannot** produce its own light now.
candle		

119

2 Think of other nouns which relate to the headings in the table. Look around your classroom for inspiration. Which column do you think will contain the most entries? Why?

3 Read these sentences. Can you spot the main verbs and the modal verbs? With your partner, try swapping the modal verbs around in the sentence. How does it change the meanings?

- *You must never play with matches.*
- *You should be very careful with electricity.*
- *This light bulb may work and it may not.*

Extra challenge

Here are some examples of modal auxiliaries: *should, must, will, could, would*. Use these words to write a safety guide on how to use the scientific equipment in school. Think about the importance of each instruction and the likelihood of things happening before you choose your modal verbs.

Project 13 – Light in our lives

Let's write

Write three paragraphs in your journal. Each paragraph should cover one of the headings from the visual organiser in the "Research and study skills" lesson. Plan your paragraphs using topic sentences like these:

> As a class, we have researched a number of facts. The speed of light as 300 million metres per second.

> However, there are some ideas that are not so objective. Scientists report that nothing travels faster than the speed of light, but how do we know this is a fact if we do not know everything?

> As we move forward, there are some further areas we would like to explore. Does light travel at the same speed across universes?

Project 14

Speaking and listening

1 Your teacher will read aloud the text below twice. Cover the text whilst you listen and fill in the gaps in the following sentences.

> Light travels as waves. Only waves with certain wavelengths are visible. Certain forms of light such as X-rays, infra-red UV-rays, cannot be detected by the human eye, though there are creatures capable of discerning these wavelengths.
>
> Isaac Newton discovered that natural daylight is composed of different colours. To demonstrate this, he refracted light through a prism. The different wavelengths produce the colours of the spectrum. We most commonly see this as the seven colours of the rainbow.

1 Light travels as _____.

2 Only waves with certain _____ are visible.

3 Certain forms of light, such as _____, infra-red or UV-rays, cannot be _____ by the human eye.

4 There are creatures _____ of discerning these wavelengths.

5 Isaac Newton discovered that _____ daylight is composed of different colours.

6 To demonstrate this, he _____ light through a _____.

7 The different wavelengths produce the colours of the _____.

8 We most commonly see this as the seven colours of the _____.

Vox pops are short interviews on a specific subject with members of the public or experts in a certain field. You may have seen these shows on television before. Ask open questions that encourage a descriptive response, rather than a *yes* or *no* answer. For example: *How do you feel about …? What do you think about …? What do you know about …?*

Project 14 – Light

2. Pretend you are on a vox pop programme called *Science Matters*. Decide on the topics you will focus on. Discuss the kinds of questions that could be asked. Will all your questions be factual or will some be opinions? As a class, prepare a list of questions.

3. Role play walking around the classroom, holding a microphone and asking different students the prepared questions on the list. The interviewers should listen to the responses of their classmates and decide on the appropriateness according to the following headings.

Uses Standard Jamaican English (SJE)?	Uses accurate vocabulary?	Answers the question fully?	Facts or opinions?

ICT opportunity

Use a camera or a microphone to record the interviews. If access is allowed, you could use a smartphone to record the interactions. Search for a camera 🎥 or mic 🎤 icon on the phone and press **record**.

Play back some of the interviews as a class so that you can analyse the language and the factual responses in more detail.

Term 2 Unit 1

Word builder

1 Match the technical words to the correct definitions.

1 visible   a an effect that alters appearance

2 spectrum   b can be detected by the human eye

3 wavelength   c the process by which plants turn light into energy

4 distortion   d a picture made from light

5 photosynthesis   e the antonym of *visible*

6 photograph   f a measure of the light frequency

7 invisible   g the range of visible colours

2 Create a word search, interconnecting as many of the topic words as possible. For example:

						r
						e
						f
						l
		c				e
		o				c
		l	i	g	h	t
		o				
		u				
p	r	i	s	m		

124

3. Use a dictionary to look up as many words with the prefix *photo-* as you can. Display these words on the board. Can you spot the link between all the *photo-* words? Write down what you think the prefix means.

4. Look in science books or online to find a range of science technical vocabulary on the topic of light. Create a mini glossary to display in the classroom.

Extra challenge

Choose a wide range of vocabulary about light and write clues to challenge students in your class. For example:

a picture taken with a camera _ _ _ _ _ _ _ _ _ _

(10 letters – *photograph*)

Term 2 Unit 1

Let's read

1. Read the statements in the table below and complete the "Before reading" column with your prediction about whether the statements are true (T) or false (F).

    Discuss your predictions with your partner or as a class and give reasons why you think your ideas might be true or false.

Before reading	Statement	After reading
	Light is required for sight.	
	Reflection is when light's direction is reversed.	
	Refraction is when light cannot pass through a material.	
	The Moon changes shape as it orbits the Earth.	
	Translucent materials reflect all the light that reaches them.	
	Animals can create light.	
	Telescopes shine light onto distant objects.	
	The reason some animals can see in the dark is because their eyes produce light.	

2. Scan the headings in the text titled *All about light*. With your partner, discuss where you would find the evidence to support the statements in Activity 1. Now read those sections to complete the "After reading" column. Write *true* or *false* bearing in mind what you have now read. Were you correct the first time around?

3. Create diagrams that illustrate the behaviour of light in the following situations. Refer to the text to find the information you need:
    - a light source shining on a transparent object
    - a light source shining on a translucent object
    - light refracted as it moves from air into water.

Project 14 – Light

All about light

Visibility

In the absence of light, nothing is visible. The light passes through the eye's pupil and is sensed by optic nerves. Some animals can see in very low light conditions, but in total darkness, sight is completely impossible.

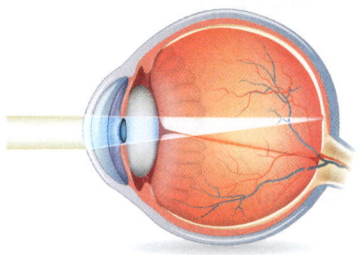

Scientific instruments

Telescopes use lenses to focus distant light.

Microscopes use a similar technique, but in this case the lens is reversed.

Modern digital cameras capture light which passes through a lens and is focused onto electronic detectors.

Reflection

When light hits a mirror or other reflective surface, the light wave returns in an opposite direction.

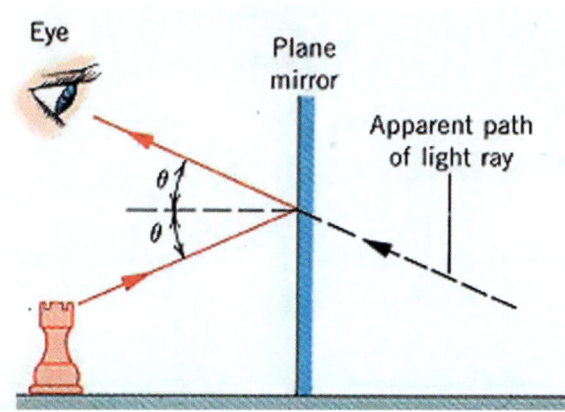

Light in the solar system

The major light source in the solar system is the Sun. Other objects can appear to change shape, but this is because the angle of reflection changes as they orbit one another. Objects such as the Moon and the planets are visible only because they reflect the Sun's rays.

Passing through materials

Transparent materials allow most of the light to pass directly through them, without reflection.

Translucent materials allow some of the light to pass through, while simultaneously reflecting the rest.

Refraction is when the speed of light changes as it passes from one medium to another.

Artificial light and bioluminescence

Bioluminescence is the process by which animals and plants produce light through chemical reactions. Examples of these creatures are pilot fish, glow-bugs and phytoplankton. Although some animals are bioluminescent, only humans are able to create light from fire or electricity.

Term 2 Unit 1

Grammar builder

1 Look at these two wheels. Write a sentence using a pronoun and a verb from the wheels on the topic of light. Make sure that the verb agrees with the pronoun.

For example: **He** experiment**s** with different instruments that reflect light.

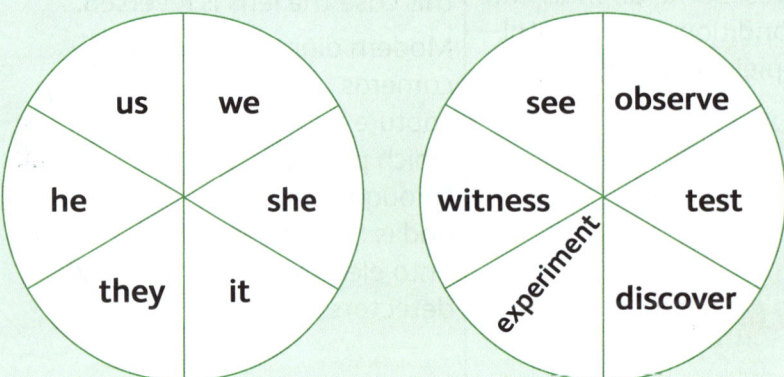

2 Now use the third wheel. This time, write a sentence using a word from each wheel on the topic of light. Do you notice anything about the main verb?

For example: **He must experiment** with the instruments before he uses them.

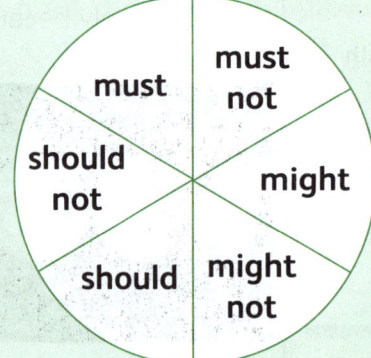

Look and learn

When you use a **modal auxiliary**, the **main verb** does not change for different pronouns. It stays in the infinitive: He **must experiment**.

Extra challenge

Write a sentence with gaps for modal auxiliaries. Use the sentence to test whether your class understands what they have learned about light.

For example: *You _____ shine light directly into your eyes from a torch.*

Project 14 – Light

Let's write

The class will work in small groups.

- Each group must think of three words to describe the behaviour of light and pass the words to the next group.
- This group must use these words to write a sentence about light.
- They then pass the words on to the next group until all groups receive their original words back.
- Each group can read out the sentences they wrote to the rest of the class.

Write a detailed, factual, organised, scientific explanation of one aspect of the behaviour of light. You could choose from the following headings:

- How does light enable us to see?
- What is the difference between reflection and refraction?
- How does light cause the phases of the moon?
- How do lenses work?

Create a diagram to support your explanation. Do the drawing first.

Now plan your paragraphs as follows.

State the problem.	Describe different opinions.	Give the correct scientific explanation.	Present a conclusion.

- Use the "Editor's checklist" for the final draft of your work and exchange your writing with a partner to give each other feedback.
- Then ask your teacher if there are further improvements you could make.

You will be writing scientifically so your writing must be in present tenses. Also make sure that the explanations are clear and use factual language, even when discussing common errors or opinions.

Editor's checklist
- present tenses
- accurate technical vocabulary
- factual and clear sentences
- organised paragraphs

Term 2 Unit 1

Project 15

 **Speaking and listening**

Your teacher will divide you into groups and assign your group one of the topics below to research as a team. The topics are from the "Let's read" lesson on light in Project 14.

- Each group member should build on their previous knowledge of the topic and extend their understanding by researching one or two new pieces of information. When your group have created their notes, you will report back to other groups researching different topics.

The topics are:
- Visibility
- Scientific Instruments
- Reflection

Remember ☆☆☆

When you take notes, you only write the key words. When you read them afterwards, the key words remind you of what you heard or read.

- Your teacher will divide you into groups where each member has researched a different topic. Use your notes to report on your topic to the new group. Other group members should listen attentively and take notes while you present your research.

Word builder

Vocabulary box

vibrate	audible	pitch
vibration	volume	frequency
audio	sonic	decibel

1. Read the passage and complete the following tasks.

> An **audible** sound is one with enough **volume** to be heard, which means that the air must have **vibrated** enough to be sensed by the ear.
>
> We measure the loudness of a sound in **decibels**, which is the unit of measure for volume.
>
> The **pitch** of a sound can be high, such as a squeak, or low such as a rumble of thunder.
>
> A sound with a high pitch has a high **frequency**, which means how quickly the air vibrates. The opposite is true for a low pitch.

1. Write a definition for each word written in bold. For example: *Audible* refers to something that can be heard.

2. Turn each of the spellings into an anagram by jumbling the letters. Challenge your partner to see who can unscramble each other's words first.

3. The words *audio* and *sonic* are technical words that refer to the topic of sound. A *sonic boom* is the sound made by an object as it travels faster than 300 metres per second, and an *audio recording* is a recording of sound rather than pictures or a video. Use a dictionary or an online resource to find other uses of the words *sonic* and *audio*.

Extra challenge

Set yourself a spelling challenge. Ask your partner to quiz you on the words. Then check your spelling. For those you got wrong, decide on a strategy to learn the correct spelling. You could set yourself a target of practicing once a day for a week. Then ask your partner to test you again to see whether you have improved.

Let's read

Read this text and complete the following tasks.

"Turn that down!"

The human ear is my favourite sense organ. It is so sensitive that the ear can detect a vibration that is one tenth the width of an atom. That's right. An atom – the smallest particle in the universe, invisible even under the strongest microscope. No wonder parents are forever yelling at their children to turn the volume down.

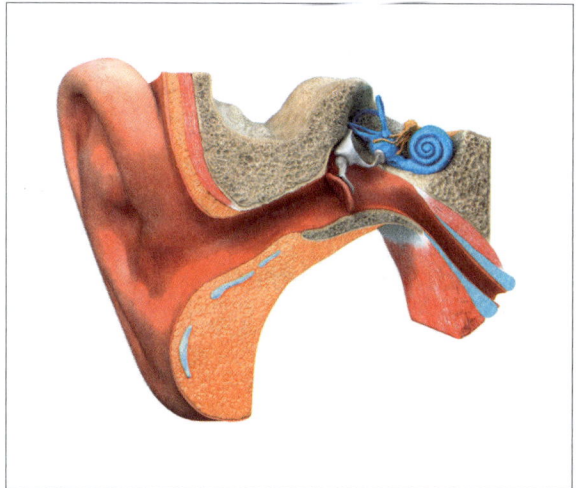

The eardrum picks up tiny vibrations in the air.

Sound is transmitted as vibrations through air, but it can also pass through solid objects, such as metal, wood, and even walls! These vibrations are picked up by the ear drum and transmitted to the brain via nerves. Many sounds do get on our nerves. Other people chewing too loudly. Someone grinding their teeth or snoring in their sleep. The barking of the neighbourhood dogs. The crying of the baby brother or sister. The buzzing of flies. All of these set us on edge.

But then, there is the other side of the equation. There are beautiful sounds which lift our spirits, like birds singing in the trees, the voices of a choir, or relaxing sounds of the waves lapping the shore. It seems the sensitivity of the ear is a blessing and a curse! The volume of a sound depends on the energy of the vibration as it travels into the ear, which is why we cover our ears if there is a loud or unpleasant noise. However, we must not forget that harsh sounds can be just as important as beautiful ones. A piercing alarm may save your life one day!

Project 15 – Sounds in our lives

1. Work in pairs to discuss the answers to the questions. Find evidence to support your claim.

Question	Answers	Evidence from text
Is the article purely factual?		
What do parents ask their children?		
How does the ear detect sound?		
Which type of sound can save your life?		
Does sound only travel through air?		
Does the author have a positive viewpoint about the topic?		

2. Skim the text titled *Turn that down!* to decide if each sentence is a fact or an opinion. Keep a tally chart like the one below. Then make an overall judgement about whether the text is objective or subjective.

Facts	Opinions
ḤḤ ḤḤ IIII	IIII
Total: 14	Total: 4

I think there will be more facts than opinions because I remember reading about scientific things like atoms and vibrations.

3. Find the phrase *the other side of the equation*. Explain what the author means by this phrase and how it is used to make the meaning clearer.

4. The author expresses astonishment at a number of facts. List these facts and explain why they could be surprising or cause amazement.

Grammar builder

Look and learn

We use tenses to talk about the past, present and future.

Past	Present	Future
Sarah ran to the shop.	Sarah runs to the shop.	Sarah will run to the shop.

We can also use the **past perfect simple**, which describes an event that has already happened.

Look at these examples:

- *I had heard the sound of the alarm.*
- *The wind had howled through the trees on that night.*
- *By lunchtime, we had forgotten everything we had been told.*

Past perfect simple is formed by using the auxiliary verb **had** before the **past participle** of the main verb. For example: *He **had** already **eaten** a sandwich before lunch.*

The past perfect is used to describe something that has already happened and been completed.

1. Which of these sentences use the past perfect simple?
   1. I hoped to see you yesterday.
   2. We had sorted all the boxes before the truck arrived.
   3. When I heard the violin, I started to cry.
   4. In January, the choir had already learned the songs.

2. Convert all of these into the past perfect simple:
   1. I saw the movie before my sister.
   2. We went to the park during the storm.
   3. You cheered me up when you smiled and waved.

3. Complete these sentences using the past perfect simple.
   1. He was late for school because he …
   2. They talked about the football match they …
   3. His parents read the school report his teacher …
   4. Her teacher was pleased with the essay she …
   5. They ate the jerk chicken their mother …

4 Find a selection of reading material. Look for examples of the past perfect simple. Write them down and then read them to the class.

5 Write a past time on a piece of paper, for example: *in February*. Ask your partner to complete the sentence using the past perfect, for example: *I had already applied to college in February.*

Term 2 Unit 1

Let's write

1. Read this passage. Then summarise the passage in two sentences. The challenge is to produce very simple, clear sentences that contain the most important message from the passage.

> Summarising a text is a very useful skill. To summarise effectively, you have to:
> - understand the main points of a text
> - explain the main points in one or two sentences
> - write very clearly and concisely.

A stringed instrument, such as a harp, produces different pitches by varying the length of each string. A shorter string produces a higher pitch due to the increased speed of vibration. Conversely, a longer string vibrates more slowly, and so generates a lower frequency. You could test this for yourself with a length of string or cotton. Hold it taut, and then pluck the string. Now shorten the length. When you pluck this time, it should give a lower pitch sound. When a guitarist or a violinist plays their musical instrument, you will see them placing their fingers on to the strings. This is to temporarily shorten the string, therefore changing the note as they play it.

2. Research other passages about the science of sounds. Examples of interesting topics could be:
   - musical instruments
   - the workings of the human ear
   - sound recording technology.

3. Select one text and compile a summary of the main points. Remember to keep a reference of the text so that your teacher and classmates can refer to it. Then share your summary with the class so that everyone can feel that they have gained some knowledge from your research!

Project 16 – The science of sound

Project 16

Speaking and listening

What would the world be like if there were no sound? What if there were only sounds, but no words?

1   Play the *Sound effect* game.

   Tell your group a story without words. You may only use sound effects. They need to tell you what you are describing in ten guesses. If they do not get it right, you can tell them.

   You could describe one of these scenarios:

   • what you did last weekend

   • what you plan to do next weekend

   • something funny that happened at school

   • something sad or scary

   • something you saw or heard on the news.

2   Play the *Window* game.

   Pretend that you can see your friend through a window. You have an urgent message to tell him or her. You attract their attention but they cannot hear you. So, you have to use actions and mime to get your message across. Your message could be:

   • something they need to collect on the way home from school

   • a warning about something dangerous outside

   • an urgent message from your teacher.

3   Pretend you are the CEO of a company that makes sound equipment, such as speakers, microphones and alarms. Give a short presentation about the importance of sound in our everyday lives. While listening to other presentations, think of some questions you could ask the speaker.

137

Word builder

1. Read the words from the vocabulary box to your partner. What do you notice?

   Vocabulary box

confession	electrician	information	decision
discussion	musician	relation	revision
profession	optician	inflation	persuasion

2. There is a pattern in the words. Explain how all of these words are related. Make a list of more words that end in *-cian*. Look them up in a dictionary to check the spelling.

3. Words that end in *-ssion* have root words that share a pattern. For example: *confess, discuss, profess*. Find more words that share this pattern.

ICT opportunity

A traditional dictionary is not very useful when you want to look up word endings. The internet is a far better resource. With your teacher's support and supervision, try the following search: *words ending in -ssion* or *list words ending in -ssion*.

Remember, we have to make sure we are sensible when we are online. Refer to the "Speaking and listening" lesson in Project 1 for online safety rules.

4. Listen very carefully to the pronunciation of these words: *decision, revision, persuasion*.

   The *-sion* is pronounced differently from the other suffixes. How would you describe the difference?

   Extra challenge

   What are some other combinations of letters that represent multiple sounds?

5. Pronunciation in English is not always easy to guess from the spelling of a word. This is because one letter or a combination of letters can represent different sounds. Think of the many different ways of pronouncing *-ough* in the following words: *rough, through, thorough, though, bough*.

Let's read

The Space Walk

Brianna opened her eyes and looked around her. She was looking back at the Earth, framed by endless space- millions of stars separated by the deepest black sky. Each one was a giant ball of gas creating its own light, just like our own Sun. It was the most amazing thing! "That's funny," she thought to herself, "I don't remember going into space!". As she moved her eyes, she noticed the vivid blues and greens of Earth

reflected in the glass in front of her eyes. She looked down and gazed at the thick, white gloves covering her hands. At least she was wearing a spacesuit, even if she couldn't remember putting it on.

She spun slowly, shifting her focus to the rope-like tether connecting her to the spacecraft. Just then, a crackling sound echoed through her helmet. "Brianna?" asked a familiar voice. It was her twin brother, Nathan. "Have you fixed the connector yet?" For the first time, she noticed a spanner in her hand. "I… I think so," she replied. "Everything looks properly connected up, but I'm not sure." Brianna couldn't even remember the trip to space, let alone how to repair a spacecraft! "Let's bring you in, then we can check…" Nathan's voice trailed off. "Whoa, look at that, Brianna!" he said, his voice filled with awe. Brianna twirled weightlessly to look back towards their home planet. A meteor with a fiery tail was streaking through the Earth's atmosphere. It was beautiful, but silent. Brianna watched the rock burning until it disappeared, but it never made a sound.

Brianna closed her eyes for a moment. When she opened them again, she was staring at her bedroom ceiling. Morning light poured in through the curtains, but this time there was no glass helmet visor to reflect it. What a strange dream! She ran to tell Nathan about it. "Space was amazing, and you were helping me!" she grinned. "The weird part was, we were quite close to the meteor, and there was so much fire, but we didn't hear a thing!" Nathan smiled back at her. "Your brain was remembering our science lesson yesterday," he said, "don't you remember? Mrs Roberts told us that light can travel through space, but sound needs a solid, liquid or gas to travel through." Brianna looked surprised. "That lesson must have really stuck in my head…' she said. "I can't wait to get to school and tell Mrs Roberts all about it!"

1   1   Look at the title and picture before you read the story. Make two predictions about details or plot (the things that will happen) in the story.

    2   Read the text carefully. Were your predictions correct? Were there any differences between your predictions and what happened in the story?

2   Write a two-sentence summary explaining what happens in this story.

3   Write one example of a fact found in the text. Then, write one example of a fictional story detail or opinion.

> **L👀k and learn**
>
> Many stories use fictional (non-real) characters, settings or details. They can also use a mixture of fact and fiction, such as a story set in pre-independence Jamaica about a fictional character. These stories can be a good way to share real information about a place, event or person in an entertaining way.

4   Were there any clues in the story that Brianna was dreaming? What were they?

5   How do you think that Brianna's teacher will react when she hears about Brianna's dream? Explain your ideas.

Grammar builder

Look and learn

Demonstrative pronouns are used to point to and refer to nouns that describe places, animals or things, and also people when the person is identified.

- For a singular thing that is near, we use the demonstrative pronoun **this**.
- For plural things that are near, we use the demonstrative pronoun **these**.
- For something that is far, we use the demonstrative pronoun **that**.
- For plural things that are far, we use the demonstrative pronoun **those**.

1 Complete the text with the correct demonstrative pronouns.

Sunlight, the stars, volcanoes and lightning are all natural sources of light. _____ types of light are not man-made but occur naturally. Sunlight is one of the most obvious sources of natural light. _____ provides a large amount of light for people to see by on a daily basis.

2 Compare your answers with a partner. With your partner, write your own short text with at least two demonstrative pronouns missing. Use the previous activity to guide you.

3 Join another pair of students. With your partner, complete each other's texts with the correct demonstrative pronoun.

4 Complete the sentences with the correct demonstrative pronouns.

1. Lloyd was late for class again. _____ boy is not going to pass his exams.

2. I love mango and coconut ice cream. _____ are my favourite flavours.

3. Can I open my present now? Wow, _____ is a lovely gift, thank you.

4. Bob Marley's first songs were great. _____ songs were the best.

Let's write

In the last project, you practised writing a summary. In this project, you are going to learn to write a detailed paragraph.

Write a detailed explanation of how sound is caused, travels through the air and is heard by a human ear.

1. Discuss this series of images. Think of one sentence to summarise each stage.

2. You will explain how sound travels, using the images above to guide you. Write an introductory paragraph that sets the tone of the piece. The language and style should make it very clear that it is a scientific, objective explanation.

3. Use the diagrams to form the basis of one paragraph for each stage of the process. Make sure you use causal conjunctions and linking phrases.

4. Once you have completed your paragraph, create or adapt each diagram to support your writing. Then edit your work by referring to the "Editor's checklist".

I will need to think carefully about the vocabulary and tense I will use to write in this style.

Editor's checklist

- Standard Jamaican English (SJE) in present tenses
- causal conjunctions and linking phrases
- organised paragraphs
- captions for each diagram

Project 17

Speaking and listening

1. Your teacher will read a poem one line at a time. Repeat each line as you hear it. This is called **echoing**.

   Listen for:
   - rhythm – stressed and unstressed words
   - volume – how loudly or quietly someone speaks
   - intonation – how the speaker's voice goes up or down.

Catherine Wheel Hurricane

A hurricane is striking, like the stick in its name
With increasing circles, like a spinning top game.
It sucks and lashes, while expanding its frame
And consuming all, in its circular domain.

What whipping wind whirls with wielding weight
As its Catherine Wheel eats the land as if bait,
Mingled with jagged piercing light,
inviting a roar of equalling spite.

But still no thunder, just circling doom
No wait, here it comes, the aftermath boom.

by Heather Raymond, 2021

Look and learn

Intonation is about the way we stress certain words or syllables. It is a very strong part of the rhythm and music of poetry. Say these words: *Jamaica, music, reflection, invisible, international*.

Can you hear that each word has its own rhythm? When we say a syllable or a word more strongly than another, we say we "stress" that part.

2 Now take it in turns to lead and repeat in an echo reading. Try these variations to explore the different ways of reading a poem:

- Read the poem one sentence at a time. Ignore the line endings and pause only at a comma or a full stop.
- Exaggerate the pitch of your tone. Lift you voice higher and lower.
- Relish the sound of each word. Feel the richness of each word and pronounce it fully.

3 In pairs, learn the poem by heart, then record each other performing the poem. Use a camera or a microphone to record the interviews. If access is allowed you could use a smartphone to record the interactions. Search for a camera or mic icon on the phone and press **record**.

Play some of the performances of students reading aloud the poem as a class so that you can analyse the rhythm, volume and intonation of your classmates in more detail.

Word builder

1 Read the following phrases and the "Remember" box.
- as clear as day
- quick like lightning
- as loud as thunder

Remember ☆☆☆

There are many examples of similes. **Similes** are a descriptive technique, like metaphors. The best similes and metaphors are surprising and familiar at the same time. If a simile is used too often, then it loses its power and becomes a cliché. The best writers and poets will use similes in a way that creates a picture of sound in your mind to enhance your understanding.

2 The similes in Activity 1 are used too often and therefore become too obvious to catch your attention. Can you bring these similes back to life? Complete the simile starter with your own ideas and then compare your completed phrases with a partner.

1. As clear as …
2. Quick like …
3. As loud as …

3 With your partner, discuss new comparisons you could make that would help your reader create more interesting pictures in their mind. Try to be inventive, fresh and interesting.

4 Play a class game, *Pass on the Similes*. A student will be given a baton and will start the game. Whoever has the baton must choose a simile starter and complete it in an interesting way. Choose from these similes:

- as quiet as …
- as silent as …
- as bright as …

The student then passes the baton on to the next student, who must create a variation of the simile. Keep going until no one can think of a new simile. Then restart the game with a new simile starter.

Example:

as quiet as a mouse

as quiet as a feather falling

as quiet as …

Let's read

1. Before reading this extract from a story titled *Sounds of the Invisible*, consider these questions:

   1. Does the title give you any clues about what might happen?
   2. Is this extract from the beginning, middle or end of the story?
   3. Can you predict what will happen next?

2. Read the extract carefully. Then return to the questions. Explain your answer to each question, using evidence from the text to support your ideas.

Sounds of the Invisible

"Be quiet!" I hissed, hoping desperately to hush my brother's chatter.

He looked sulky for a moment, then remembered why we were hiding, and hunkered down into the grass. I knew he would be unable to stay quiet for long, but I leaned forward until I was close to the edge and strained my ears. After a while, just when Jonah was beginning to fidget again, I thought I caught the faintest scuffle, the crunch of footsteps on the path.

I tapped my brother and told him what I was thinking with my eyes. I jerked my head in the direction of the path and put my fingers slowly to my lips. Jonah's eyes opened wide, and he took a deep gulp of air. I realised that I too was holding my own breath.

As the sound got closer, something caught me quite by surprise. There were footsteps of more than one person. More than two. More than ten! As the sounds approached, I could see nothing, but the sounds grew louder and louder, and more numerous. Surely, I thought, nothing but a whole army could make this kind of noise. I put my hand to my chest to see if the rattling of my heart against my ribs could be adding to the din. Jonah was frozen, eyes wider still. I looked down and saw that his legs were coiled, ready at any moment to spring from his place and charge. I could not guess which way he would go: headlong into trouble, or away. Away, away, away, never to look back.

3 What can you infer about Jonah? Find clues in the text that tell us about Jonah's personality, characteristics, appearance and emotions.

4 How does the narrator communicate with Jonah without using sounds? Find three examples in the text and discuss why he chooses to communicate in this way.

5 Develop some questions of your own about the text. They should fall into these categories:

   1 Questions from the text: ask specific questions about word choice and word meaning from the text.

   2 Questions that require inference: ask questions that require the reader to consider the scenario and the personality or thoughts and feelings of the narrator.

   3 Questions for the author: ask questions that only the author would be able to answer about the effects and purpose of the text.

> ### What's your view?
> This text is written in the first person (from the narrator's point of view). Why might authors sometimes choose to use the first person instead of the third person?

Grammar builder

1. One person should read a passage from a text aloud to the rest of the class. While listening, the class should close their eyes and let the words paint pictures and play sounds in their minds.

Extra challenge

Your teacher may choose the first passage to be read aloud, but you may have an idea for a different passage. Have you read a story or a poem that vividly painted a picture for you? If yes, suggest this passage be used to repeat the activity. You could even volunteer to be the one who reads aloud to everyone else.

2. When the reading is finished, the class should sketch what mental images came to mind. The sketches do not need to be perfect – just representations of what images the words created as they were spoken.

3. Annotate your sketch using the following parts of speech:
   - nouns
   - adjectives
   - verbs.

   Make your word choices and descriptions as precise and vivid as you can.

4. Create some similes to annotate your sketch. These similes should bring the pictures and the setting to life. Try to think of similes that work for each of the senses.

5. Compare your sketches and annotations with a partner. What is the same and what is different? Are you surprised by anything in your partner's sketch?

Let's write

1. Write a story on light or sound. Discuss the following diagram of a story's structure.

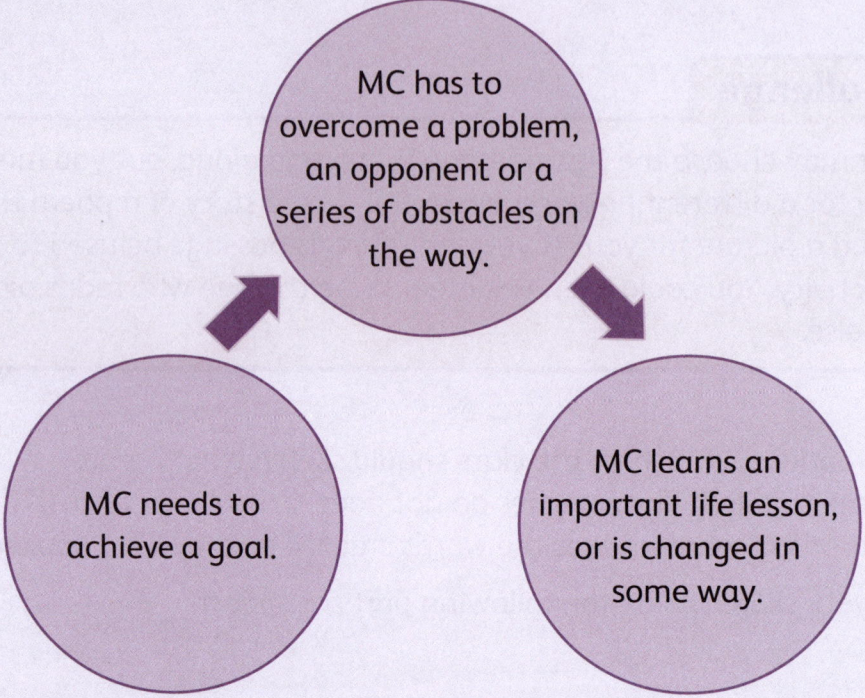

2. What do you think MC stands for? Think of a well-known story or movie. Explain how it fits into this structure.

3. Discuss the following questions:

   1. Which part of the story contains the most descriptions?

   2. Where would you expect to use dialogue?

   3. How can you help the reader understand the flow from one part of the story to another?

4. Use the writing process to produce your own story. As a class, brainstorm ideas for stories on the topic of light and sound. You may like to start by thinking about the ideas you had when reading the extract *Sounds of the Invisible* in your "Let's read" lesson.

Project 17 – Sounds of science

Planning

Sketch a diagram like the story diagram above.

- In the first circle, plan your main character and the goal they will need to achieve.
- In the second circle, plan the obstacle they will need to overcome. This could be an external obstacle, like an opponent or a dangerous journey, but it could also be an internal obstacle, like fear, pride or anger.
- In the third circle, plan the ending of the story. Pay attention to what the main character will have learned.

Organise your paragraphs. You could write your paragraph openers first, and then think of any writing techniques you can use to enhance the writing. Now write your first draft.

	Opening sentence	Adjectives and nouns	Verbs and adverbs	Synonyms
Beginning				
Middle				
End				

Remember ☆☆☆

Remember when you thought of different ways to begin a story in Term 1, Unit 1. Review the different types of story opening and decide if one would work well in your second draft.

Editor's checklist

Re-read your story and check against:

- Does my story have figurative language such as similes?
- Does my story have organised paragraphs?
- Does my story have a clear beginning, middle and end?

Project 18

Speaking and listening

Listen to a piece of music. Your teacher may choose the first one, but some of the class may have suggestions as well.

ICT opportunity

The BBC have a project called *Ten Pieces* that brings classical music from around the world to life. Your teacher may choose to use some of these clips. There are also clips of orchestras from around the world playing some of the most evocative pieces of music ever written.

1. Close your eyes while you listen to the music. Let the sounds paint pictures and notice what feelings bubble up while you listen. Listening to music can be one of the most emotional experiences ever.

2. When the music finishes, listen again, but this time sketch the pictures it paints as you listen. You might also start to annotate with nouns, verbs, adjectives and similes.

3. Discuss your opinions of the music. This kind of discussion can become very heated! Some people can become offended if their favourite music is criticised by someone else.

4. Look back at the communication protocol that you produced at the beginning of this unit, in Project 13. Discuss how to adapt it to include how to show respect for an idea or opinion that you disagree with.

5. Listen to some pieces of music from different genres. Discuss the following:

    1. What is your opinion of the music?

    2. Can you apply your understanding of the science of sound to your appreciation of the piece?

    3. How do the different rhythms and pitches affect the "meaning" of the piece?

Project 18 – Sound and light in movies

Word builder

1. Look back over all the topic words in this unit. Make a list and organise them into groups according to the following categories:
   - sound or light
   - easy or difficult.

2. Use the words and spellings in Activity 1 for the following activities.

Meanings
- Create a matching game. Choose ten words and write a definition for each word.
- Challenge a partner to match the definition to the correct word.

Extra challenge
Also include homonym definitions. For example, *light* means visible waves, but also how heavy something is.

Extra challenge
Create some "Top Five" lists:
Top five trickiest spellings
Top five words with more than three syllables

Prefixes, suffixes and root words
Look for as many words as you can that begin with these prefixes:
- *photo-*
- *tele-*
- *micro-*.

Extra challenge
Now try for words with these suffixes:
- *-ic*
- *-scope*
- *-graph*.

My grammar skills

Spelling patterns
Create mnemonics and other strategies for remembering the common misspellings of the words. Begin with the following:
- colour
- prism
- audible
- vision.

Extra challenge
Use a computer to create a class blog of the strategies that can help you learn the trickiest words.

Quizzes
Create one of the following to help everyone else practise this unit's spellings:
- anagram challenge
- wordsearch
- find the mistake
- flashcards.

Extra challenge
Design a crossword with clues ranging from simple to difficult.

Let's read

Read the following music review.

Song for you

This band have been going from strength-to-strength recently. Just two years ago, they almost broke up and were considering hanging up their guitars for good. Thank goodness they didn't!

This is the kind of music that brings a smile to your face, even when the world is against you. It is as if they have captured the sunbeams that warm your face and turned them into notes and lyrics. I first heard this song on the radio when I was stuck in a traffic jam. I could not help myself – I sang as loud as a wolf howling to the moon, and I did not care who heard me or saw me.

If you are feeling down, then this is the song for you. If you need to cheer up your friend whose pet goldfish has just died – this is the song. If you have watched the news any time in the last year, then THIS IS THE SONG FOR YOU!

This extract was posted on a website for a music magazine. Here are some of the comments from the website:

---

mysearch.jm | Jamaican Creole

5 minutes ago
Sea_breezy: Fool fool music like dat fi stap play pon di radio!

1 minute ago
Reply:
Multicultural4evs: Yu so negative! Di song uplifting but you cyan see dat cause you blindid by di sang dem bout faas cyar an girls an money.

18 minutes ago
DMighty: Mi love deh song yah. It mek me feel gud every time mi hear it.

22 minutes ago
Dino: Dem kinda tune yah di yute dem fi hear. Bless up!

40 minutes ago
Kells: Kmt. Unuh cyan feel good pon unuh own?

1 Find five different words or phrases from the article that clearly show the author's point of view.

2 Identify the following persuasive techniques that the author has used:
   - repetition
   - appeal to emotions
   - painting pictures with words
   - humour.

3 Choose three of the examples you found in the text for Activity 3. Imagine that the review was about a sad song instead of a happy one. How could you change your chosen examples to show this?

4 This review is from a music magazine. Why might readers choose to learn about other people's point of view in this way?

5 Read the comments again. Sort them into categories of positive and negative. Compare and contrast the persuasive techniques used by the different commentors.

Grammar builder

1. This is a review of the grammar you have learned in this unit. There are four main areas. Work with a partner or in a group to think about each area.

Similes	Parts of speech
Complete the following similes in five different ways: • as reflective as … • as thunderous as … • bright like … Use them to describe a monster.	Using a photograph or a painting, write as many of the following to describe the image: • nouns • verbs • adjectives • adverbs of time, place or manner
Synonyms	**Comparing and contrasting words**
Make a list of words that you use frequently, such as *nice*, *good*, *happy*, *bad* and find at least three synonyms for each. Work with a partner who has to remind you to use a synonym every time you insert the frequently used words in your speech.	Create a class list or glossary of comparing and contrasting words and phrases. Include examples of each being used as a reminder of how to use them correctly. Display the lists in your classroom and add to them over time as new comparing and contrasting words and phrases are learned. Remember to use these words in your speech and writing when appropriate!

2. When you have finished your grammar check, come back together as a class. You will look at the four boxes again with your teacher. Be ready to share the responses and examples that you come up with in your group.

Extension task

Write a short paragraph or a few sentences that demonstrates all of the grammar skills from this unit. Your teacher may choose yours to be published on the school website as an example of the learning from your class this term.

Self-check

- How confident are you about using each of the grammar skills?
- List the skills and draw the emoji that matches how you feel about each skill.

Grammar	☹	OK	👍
Similes			
Parts of speech			
Present perfect			
Modal auxiliaries			

Project 18 – Sound and light in movies

Let's write

Imagine you work for a magazine website that reviews new music and new movies. It is your job to produce informative reviews that people want to read to find out if they should watch a new movie, download some new music or go to a music concert.

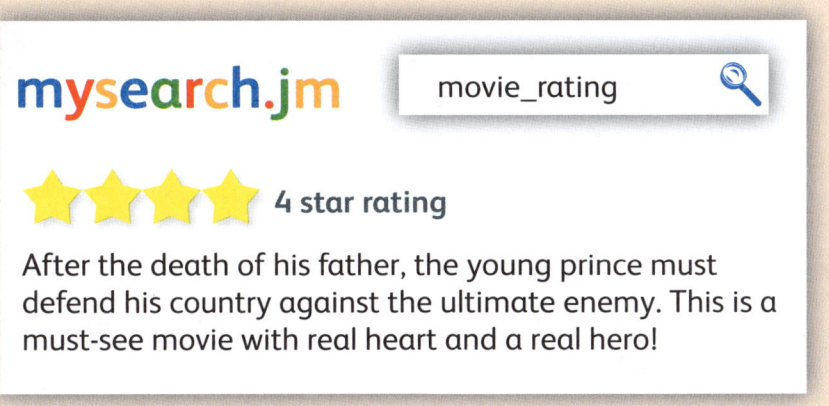

After the death of his father, the young prince must defend his country against the ultimate enemy. This is a must-see movie with real heart and a real hero!

1. Choose the music or the movie you will review. Think about the following:

   - The best movie you have seen in the last year.
   - A movie you saw which nearly sent you to sleep.
   - The song your brother or sister has listened to so many times that you would rather never hear again. Ever!
   - A piece of music that makes you dance, laugh or cry and that you think everyone in the world should listen to.

2. Plan some words or phrases that you can use to express your viewpoint about the song or movie. Use a mind map to help you think of different ideas:

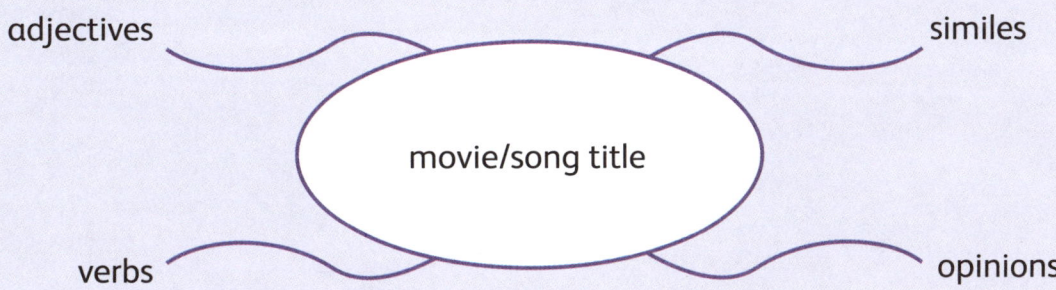

157

3 Plan your paragraphs:

Introduce the piece.	Describe the genre or the basic plot.	Describe the effect it has when you watch or listen.	Compare and contrast with other movies or songs.	Conclusion – overall rating and recommendation (or not).

4 Check your completed review against the "Editor's checklist".

Editor's checklist
- Does the review use persuasive techniques?
- Does the review include viewpoints?
- Did you include features of a review article?

Term 2 Unit 1 Review and assessment

Word builder

1. One word in each sentence sounds the same. Identify that word and then decide whether it is a noun or an adjective. Circle the noun and underline the adjective. The first one is done for you.

   1. This housing (complex) needs to be refurbished before the new tenants are invited to move in.

      This is a very complex situation and we will need time to think about it.

   2. Give me a second and I will be right there!

      That was the second time that he was reminded to take his textbook to school.

   3. Do not make any rash decisions; you will have to live with this for years to come.

      The doctor said the rash should disappear after a few applications of the ointment.

   4. I am thinking about my career path and I need some expert advice.

      Dr John is an expert at career placement.

   5. Kelly left the key inside the house and now we cannot get in without a locksmith.

      A key ingredient is missing from this dish; it tastes different when Mom makes it.

Let's read

1. Read the extract from the poem *South* by Kamau Brathwaite and answer the following questions.

   1. But today I recapture the islands'
   2. bright beaches: blue mist from the ocean
   3. rolling into the fishermen's houses.
   4. By these shores I was born: sound of the sea

5   came in at my window, life heaved and breathed in me then

6   with the strength of that turbulent soil.

2   The word *capture* means *to take hold of something*. What do you think the poet means by the word *recapture*? What is the poet recapturing?

3   Why do you think the mist is blue?

4   Identify the alliteration in line 2.

5   Identify the alliteration in line 4.

6   Tick (✓) the correct answer. The line "sound of the sea came in at my window" is an example of:

☐ a simile – uses the words *like* or *as* to make a comparison

☐ a metaphor – states the comparison without using *like* or *as*

☐ personification – to assign human qualities to an object.

Grammar builder

The past perfect simple is used to describe something that has already happened and been completed.

1   Which of these sentences use past perfect tenses?

   1   I wanted to meet you this morning.

   2   We had already finished eating before Tom finally arrived.

   3   When I arrived at the beach, I immediately started to swim.

   4   It had been raining, but the sun is now shinning.

2   Convert these sentences using the past perfect simple.

   1   I ate all the biscuits before my sister came home.

   2   We saw the movie before my friends.

   3   You helped me to revise, that's why I passed.

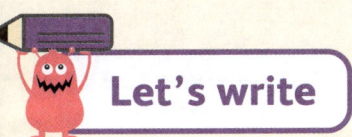

Let's write

Read the text. Then write a paragraph about an experience where sound has been a blessing or a curse for you.

> There are beautiful sounds which lift our spirits, like birds singing in the trees, a choir singing, or relaxing sounds of the waves lapping the shore. It seems the sensitivity of the ear is a blessing and a curse! The volume of a sound depends on the energy of the vibration as it travels into the ear, which is why we cover our ears if there is a loud or unpleasant noise. However, we must not forget that harsh sounds can be just as important as beautiful ones. A piercing alarm may save your life one day!

TERM 2 — Unit 2

Project 19

Speaking and listening

1. Look at the diagrams. Discuss with the class how muscles and bones work to enable the human body to move.

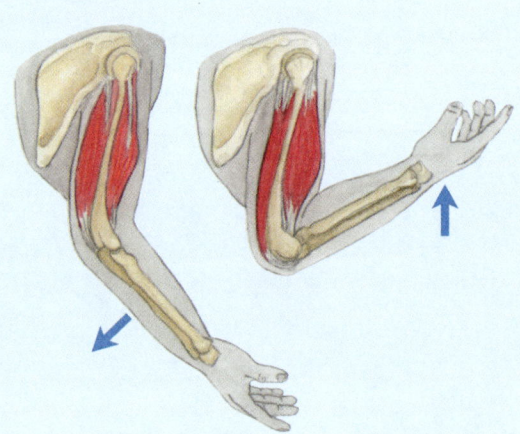

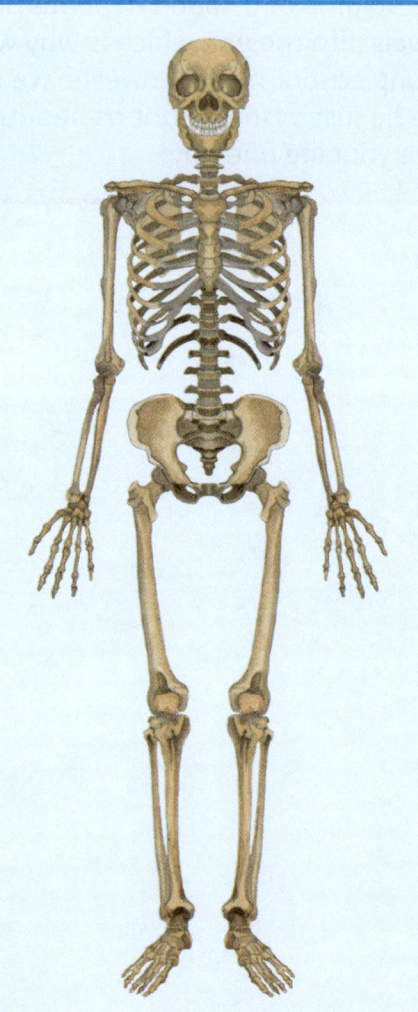

2. In groups, create a role play that demonstrates the different movements caused by muscles, bones and joints. For example, pick up objects, bend your knees, feel your muscles contract and relax to bring about these movements and discuss about muscles, joints and bones. The role-play should include verbal and non-verbal elements.

If you have studied the human body in your Science lessons, you could revise how the body flexes and extends various muscles whilst planning your role play.

Look and learn

Verbal cues are any spoken words that prompt a response.

Non-verbal cues are pictures, actions and sounds that do not use words.

Project 19 – The way we move

Word builder

1. Read the words from the vocabulary box to a partner. These are all technical words and are linked to the topic of movement in the human body. Use the technique of syllabification to determine the correct pronunciation. For example: *syl-lab-i-fi-ca-tion = six syllables*.

Vocabulary box

- muscle
- muscular
- skeleton
- skeletal
- tendon
- anatomy
- ligament
- musculoskeletal
- orthopaedic

There are often disagreements about the best way to split a word into syllables. With your teacher's approval, you could confirm the number of syllables in a word by listening to someone online sound it out. This is often indicated with a speaker icon 🔊.

2. Choose two words from the vocabulary box and ask your partner to describe the difference between them. For example:

What's the difference between *muscle* and *muscular*?

Muscle is a noun. It is a mass of tissue that helps us to move our bones. *Muscular* is an adjective used to describe something relating to muscles. For example, *Athletes have muscular bodies.*

L👀k and learn

Words have a history. The history of how a word came to mean what it does today is called **etymology**. You might be surprised to learn that the word we use for *muscle* comes from a Latin word meaning *little mouse*. Can you imagine why that would be?

> **Extension task**
> Etymology is about the origin of words and how their meaning has changed over time.
> Use an internet search with your teacher to look for the etymology of *muscle*, *skeleton* and *anatomy*.

3   Think about your role play in the "Speaking and listening" lesson. In pairs, write sentences using the technical vocabulary from the word list.

Project 19 – The way we move

Let's read

Read the text titled *Training the body to move*.

Training the body to move

When you watch a dancer, a gymnast or perhaps an athlete, their movements can appear effortless and natural. The truth is, they will have spent many hundreds or thousands of hours training their bodies to be able to move with such strength and control.

The body's movement depends upon the joints being used effectively. There are different types of joint in the body. The knee and the elbow are examples of hinge joints. These allow movement in one direction, out and back. The shoulder is an example of a ball-and-socket joint. These joints allow movement up to 360-degree rotations. There are other types of joints too, including those in the fingers and thumbs, and those in the spine and neck. The spinal joints are very important and must be protected and exercised with caution.

Athletic injuries occur where a muscle is overstretched, or where a joint is forced to move in a way it is not supposed to. The hamstring is a muscle located in the back of the thigh, and hamstring strains are a common muscle injury. A dislocation is an injury where a joint is damaged and one of the bones is pulled or pushed out of the correct position. To avoid injuries such as these, dancers, athletes and gymnasts perform warm-ups and develop their movements gradually, with control.

1. Read the text again and complete the 3-2-1 table to summarise your understanding of the text.

3 Things I know	2 Things I found interesting	1 question I have

2. Share your responses with the class. Can working as a group answer some of your questions and help deepen everyone's understanding?

Research and study skills

As you progress with your studies, you will need to back up your ideas and opinions with evidence. Evidence is stated and sometimes implied which means it is suggested and not directly stated. When you have your evidence, you then have to evaluate the effectiveness of those ideas in the texts.

Make an evaluation of the effectiveness of the text *Training the body to move*.

1 What is its purpose?

2 Has the text achieved its purpose?

    1 Is the text explained well or should there be more examples?

    2 Are there sufficient text features (a title, headings, subheadings, bold text, etc.) to bring clarity to the text?

3 Does the text leave too many questions unanswered, or was there enough information?

4 What would you do to make this text more effective? Compare your answers with a partner. Discuss your evaluation and the reasons for any differences of opinion.

Grammar builder

Remember ☆☆☆

Demonstrative adjectives are used to point to a particular noun. For example:
*I have a pain in **these** muscles.*

Demonstrative pronouns are used in the place of a specific noun. For example:
*I cannot move **this**.*

1. Locate any demonstrative pronouns or adjectives in the text titled *Training the body to move* that you studied in the "Let's read" lesson.

2. In pairs, add a selection of demonstrative pronouns and demonstrative adjectives to the following text.

The joints in the knees and elbows are similar. The elbow and knee joints are called *hinge joints*. Ligaments and tendons hold the knee and elbow joints together and join muscles to the bones. The muscles in the legs are called *hamstrings* and *calves*. The hamstrings and calves are layered muscles that give an athlete power to run and jump. Movements of running and jumping are used in sports and gymnastics. Muscles in the arms are called *biceps* and *triceps*. Biceps and triceps work in opposition to create upper body strength. Upper body strength is important for lifting and carrying, though other muscles in the back are also required for lifting and carrying.

ICT opportunity

Create a short presentation using slides which shows how pronouns can be used to replace nouns. Presentation applications usually allow for simple animations. You could use this feature to demonstrate how pronouns replace nouns and how demonstrative adjectives are usually inserted before a noun. Search online or ask your teacher for step-by-step instructions on how to create animations or transitions on PowerPoint.

- Remember, you must be sensible online. Refer to the "Speaking and listening" lesson in Project 1 for online safety rules.

Let's write

You are going to write a story starting with the sentence below. The theme of the story is human movement.

"It was just yesterday I thought I would never have this experience. As soon as I entered the room, all eyes were fixed on me. I was …"

1. Use the following writing process:
   - planning
   - first draft
   - checking
   - re-drafting.

Which parts of the process do you think is the most important? Discuss this as a class and share your thoughts on how you would approach each process.

Remember ☆☆☆

A **storyboard** is a set of boxes or other shapes placed in an order for the writer to put information, pictures, symbols or text.

2. Follow each stage in the writing process below.

Planning	First draft
Use a storyboard to map out the beginning, middle and end of the story.	Begin with topic sentences for each paragraph, then complete the details using description, action and dialogue.
Checking	Re-drafting
Use a writer's checklist to consider: • Accuracy – is the writing clear and appropriate? • Engagement – is the reader going to become involved in the story? • RAFT – does it meet these requirements?	Consider the main areas that need improving. Choose alternative strategies for story openings.

3. Use the RAFT strategy to think about how to plan this story effectively.

   Role – What is the role of the narrator in this story?

   Audience – Who is the writing intended for? How will this affect the language choices?

   Format – What structure does this format require to be effective?

   Topic – What vocabulary and themes are central to this topic?

Project 20

Speaking and listening

1. In pairs, read aloud the ICT Opportunity to each other and complete tasks 1 and 2.

ICT opportunity

Businesses now use the internet as a major place to advertise. Sometimes, adverts that are not suitable for children may "pop-up" if you do not use the internet with caution. This is one reason why young people should use the internet under supervision, as the advertisements are designed to persuade and influence the way you think.

1. With supervision from your teacher, observe some local audio and video advertising on the internet about healthy food, exercise equipment or food supplements. Discuss the techniques used and whether the adverts are honest in their content.

2. Focus your listening using the table below. What do you notice about the major language choices used.

Phrase used	Jamaican Creole (JC)?	Standard Jamaican English (SJE)?	Effect and reason for the choice by the advertising company

L👀k and learn

Using questions to evaluate and make judgements about information you listen to or read is an important skill that helps a student become more sophisticated. These questions include:

- How effective is the piece?
- How might it be improved?
- Are there any ethical considerations?

2. As a class, discuss this opinion: *Advertising is a form of lying.*

Word builder

1 Read the list of contractions to a partner. Share your pronunciation with the class and work together to correct any pronunciation mistakes.

2 *Couldn't* is a contraction of *could not*. Complete the expansions for the remaining words above.

3 There are some common errors when using contractions. Look at the lists below and discuss strategies for how to avoid using the incorrect homophone.

- They're – there – their
- We're – were
- You're – your

Write the full form of each of these words in your notebook.

> **Extra challenge**
>
> Look at a variety of texts. For example, an email, a newspaper, a magazine, a school book, etc. Which kinds of text do not tend to use contractions? Can you explain why?

When the word *is* is used in a contraction, there can be some confusion about whether the 's represents a contraction, a possessive or a plural.

4 Discuss the following sentences and decide which one is used:

- *Brianna's my cousin.*
- *My cousin's name is Brianna.*
- *There are two Briannas in my family.*

Project 20 – Be strong and healthy

Let's read

1. Look at the advertisements. Describe the intended audience and use evidence from the texts to justify your judgements.

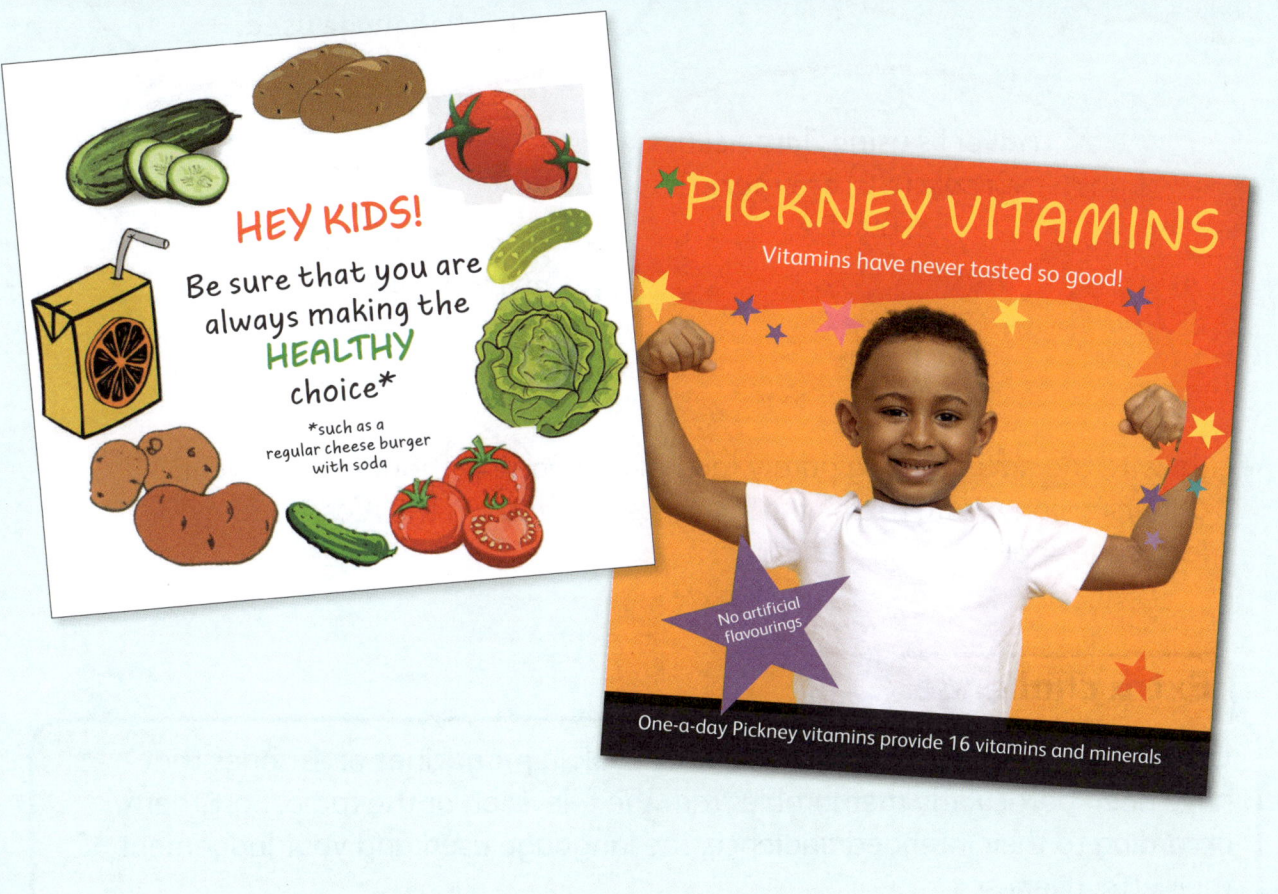

2. Complete the table for each advert. Think carefully about the author's intention behind each choice.

	Example	Standard Jamaican English (SJE) or Jamaican Creole (JC)?	Purpose/effect
Slogan			
Factual information			
Images			
Small print			

3. Discuss the following opinions in the message portrayed by the adverts.

Adverts are more about persuasion than giving information.

Non-verbal elements of adverts are even stronger than the language used.

Adverts using Jamaican Creole (JC) are more effective.

Some people are better at ignoring adverts than others.

4. Rewrite the adverts using purely factual language without any elements of persuasion. Share them with the class and explain the reasons for your language choices.

Extra challenge

Collect slogans and jingles from adverts. Look in magazines or list ones that have been particularly memorable from the television or the radio. Sort them according to their intended audience, the language used and your judgement of their effectiveness.

Project 20 – Be strong and healthy

Grammar builder

1. Read the following sentences taken from magazine articles and adverts:
   - Treat yourself to a gym membership!
   - How we can train ourselves to eat better.
   - This athlete injured herself by over-training.
   - I want to learn to be healthier, not just for myself but for my family, too.

   Identify any pronouns in the sentences.

> **Look and learn**
> Reflexive pronouns are a special kind of pronoun that refers to itself!
> It uses either *-self* or *-selves* as a suffix to indicate that it is reflexive.

2. Reflexive pronouns can be either singular (*-self*) or plural (*-selves*). Choose a suitable reflexive pronoun to complete each sentence:

   1. The problem will sort _____ out.
   2. Most problems will not sort _____ out.
   3. Andrew kept reminding _____ the reason for all the training he was doing.
   4. The team did not need to remind _____ why they were training so hard.

3. Write a sentence using each of the reflexive pronouns in Activity 2. For example: *My cat licks itself all the time.*

Can you explain why only *your* has *-self* and *-selves* as suffixes?

Extra challenge

"Reflexive pronouns are used where the action of a verb is acting on the subject of that verb."

Discuss this complicated statement. Can you create a diagram using non-verbal techniques to make this grammatical statement easier to understand? You may benefit from using example sentences and sentences which do NOT need reflexive pronouns to complete them.

Project 20 – Be strong and healthy

Let's write

1. In a small group, decide on a product or service you can advertise. The group will need to agree on this using a communication protocol.

   Remember ☆☆☆

   Communication protocol
   - Listen carefully to what everyone says.
   - Ask questions at an appropriate time.
   - Form your speech clearly and accurately so everyone can understand.
   - If you disagree, say so politely and explain why.

2. Complete the following writing tasks.

   1. Create a strong visual magazine advert, such as a poster.

   2. Create a script for a radio advert using dialogue to advertise the product effectively.

   3. Write a paragraph that appears to be an independent review of a product, but is in fact designed to advertise and persuade people that it is effective.

3. For each task, discuss the following questions.

   1. Where shall we use Jamaican Creole (JC) and where shall we use Standard Jamaican English (SJE)? What effect will the shift have?

   2. How can we use specific persuasive techniques such as:
      - slogans
      - opinions
      - rhymes or alliteration.

   3. Who is the intended audience for each piece?

4 Agree on an "Editor's checklist" for each writing task.

- One person writes the first draft.
- The second person checks the draft against the checklist you created. Create a list of constructive feedback for changes required.
- The third person makes any required changes.
- Once the piece is returned to your group, share it with the class. You could even perform the scripts.

Project 21

Speaking and listening

1. In pairs, look at these images and discuss how you think the people are overcoming adversity. Adversity could be an injury, a disability, a disease or experiencing difficult circumstances.

2. With your partner, discuss what support you think they need from the community, their family and from their country. How could these support groups improve these people's lives?

3. With your partner, join another pair of students and pool your ideas together.

4. Come together as a class to discuss the best way your community could support the people in the pictures.

Word builder

Vocabulary box

injury	paralysis	convalesce
disability	physiotherapy	rehabilitation
operation	recuperation	adversity

1 Read the words from the vocabulary box to your partner. Talk about the word meanings as you go. Discuss pronunciation and write a pronunciation guide for each word, breaking the words up into syllables. Use a dictionary to find the meanings of each of these words.

ICT opportunity

Use a computer to create a glossary of the terms in the vocabulary. The glossary should include a definition, pronunciation guide and an example of each word used in a sentence.

2 The words from the vocabulary box use the following prefixes:
- in-
- dis-
- para-
- physio-
- re-
- con-
- ad-

Look up the meaning of each prefix and complete the table.

Prefix	Meaning	Examples	Sentence using an example word
in-			

3 Select a spelling strategy to learn the correct spelling of each word, for example: syllabification, prefix + root, mnemonics or recognising common letter strings.

Let's read

1 Read the text. What does the author mean by "It is lucky we were wearing our seatbelts"?

Getting better

All I can say is, "It is lucky we were wearing our seatbelts."

The doctors told my mother and father that I probably would never walk again. They never said the word, but they feared I would be paralysed from the waist down.

I had been in a car accident – my mother was driving, and I was sitting with my brother next to me in the back seat. I remember we were arguing about what we wanted to listen to on the radio, when suddenly some bright lights shone into the car, as if a giant robot had loomed over us and was peering into the car. The next thing I remember was waking up, upside-down and all I could hear was the sound of someone sawing through wood. Only after a while did I realise it was not someone sawing, but my brother's rough breathing. His femur (that's the large bone above your knee) had been broken in three places. These days, it is pinned together. He's still the same energetic boy he ever was and runs around with just the slightest ghost of a limp. After that, I blacked out.

The next thing I remember is waking up with four worried faces staring at me: my mother, two unknown faces (who I quickly learned were doctors) and there at the foot of my bed, my brother. I had been asleep for three days! Those worried looks didn't leave their faces for many weeks.

During my rehabilitation, I discovered more about anatomy. I had to learn because of the physiotherapy that I had to do as part of my recovery. A physiotherapist is a specialist in the kinds of exercises that help you to recover from an injury, or to cope with a disability. Although my mother and father didn't tell me, I knew there was something wrong, as I couldn't move my legs at all.

People say I am a hero, that I have shown incredible bravery. I don't agree. I was never especially brave before the accident. I hated even getting a splinter – I would run and hide whenever my parents wanted to pull a plaster from my skin. No. I just had to get on with getting better. The heroes are the doctors and the physiotherapist who put me back together again, my little brother who was too young to understand everything that was happening to us, and especially my mother, who refused to accept that I would be unable to walk again.

Three years later, thanks to the love, kindness and expertise of everyone around us, I am back on my feet and once again chasing my dreams.

179

2 Answer the questions and complete the tasks.

1. What time did the accident occur? Justify your answer with evidence from the text.

2. Find and copy a phrase that suggests the narrator's injuries were severe.

3. The narrator describes her brother's breathing using a strong image. Explain the effect of this language choice.

4. Who do you think caused the accident? Can you know for sure or make a reasonable prediction?

5. Do you think the narrator is being too modest when she says she is not a hero? What is your opinion?

3 Write some questions for the narrator and her family to find out more about the accident.

4 Answer the following questions.

1. Does this text remind you of any movies or stories you have heard?

2. Have you seen anything like this on the news or in documentaries?

3. Do you know anyone who has been injured, or who has had to work to overcome a disability?

Research and study skills

1 In pairs, research about an individual who has battled a difficulty. This could be someone famous or a family member.

- Find out as much as you can about the source of their difficulty and the strength they found to overcome it.

- Find out about the support they have received from others to help them on their journey.

- Make sure you keep a record of any sources you use in your research so you can refer to them in the writing lesson when you will write a speech.

2 Use what you know about the writing process to plan a speech about their journey. You will need to think carefully about how to write the speech in a way that keeps the interest of the audience. Ask your teacher if you can carry out an internet search on the key elements of a successful speech.

3. Copy and complete the table in your notebook. You will need this information when you write your speech in the writing lesson.

R	A	F	T
Role – what is your role as speaker? Are you there to entertain, to persuade, to inform or to teach?	**Audience** – what sort of details will the audience find most engaging?	**Format** – how can you structure a speech to make it interesting and informative?	**Topic** – what vocabulary will be appropriate.

Grammar builder

Remember ☆☆☆

A subordinate clause is a clause that is introduced with a conjunction. There are different types of subordinate clauses. In this lesson, we will learn about the **relative clause**, which is introduced with a relative pronoun such as *who*, *which* or *that*.

1 Read the "Remember" box and find the relative clauses in these sentences.
   1 Sam's leg, which was broken in the accident, has been pinned together.
   2 Sam, who recovered well, can now play football again.
   3 Sam trains on Thursdays, which is convenient.
   4 They play on the pitch that was resurfaced recently.

2 Try removing the relative clause. What happens to the meaning of the sentence?

3 Choose an appropriate relative pronoun to complete these sentences.
   1 Aaliyah is one of the students _____ studies the hardest.
   2 She likes to read _____ her brother watches TV.
   3 The subject _____ she likes best is History.

4 Write sentences that use each of these relative clauses:
   1 who was born in 2001
   2 which always reminds me of my grandmother
   3 that surprised everyone who saw it
   4 while preparing for the party
   5 who did not actually know anything about how to repair engines

Extra challenge

It is important to make sure that the verb following the relative clause agrees with the subject of the sentence.
What is wrong with the following sentence? Find two mistakes.
The children, who was in the play, all need to learn their lines before the performance.

Project 21 – They overcame

Let's write

1. Refer to the writing process plan in the "Research and study skills" lesson and write a speech about the journey of an individual who has battled a difficulty. Remember, you will need to think carefully about how to write the speech in a way that keeps the interest of the audience.

2. Take some time to read the speech aloud to yourself, or to a partner. Sometimes, we do not fully realise the patterns and rhythms of our writing until we hear them being read out loud.

3. Are there any sections which need correcting, cutting or expanding further? Ask your partner to edit your speech using the following checklist.

Area of focus	Observation	Suggestion
Organisation	Not enough signal words	Use linking words like *therefore* and *less than a month later* to help the audience follow the story.
Use of Standard Jamaican English (SJE)		
Use of Jamaican Creole (JC)		
Speech performance		

183

Project 22

Speaking and listening

1. Your teacher will read the text about the digestive system twice. Cover the text, listen and answer the following questions.
   - What is the main point?
   - What are the important facts I need to be able to understand this?
   - Is there anything that I need to hear again or to discuss?

The five stages of the digestive system

There are five major stages of the digestive system and each plays an important role in ensuring that we get the nutrients from the food we eat.

The first stage is chewing. When we chew our food, it is broken into small pieces. This makes it easier for the food to be swallowed and it also helps the enzymes in our mouth to begin their work of breaking down the starches.

Swallowing is the second stage. Though we do not think about it, it involves a few processes. The tongue pushes the food towards the back of the throat where special throat muscles are waiting to push the food through the long tube, called the *oesophagus*, toward the stomach. While that is happening, a flap called the *epiglottis* closes off the windpipe to prevent the food from entering as this can lead to choking.

The third stage occurs in the stomach. The food stays in the stomach for four hours while more enzymes break down things like protein so they can be used by our bodies. The stomach is also where the bad bacteria are killed so that they do not harm our bodies.

Digestion continues with the fourth stage in the small intestines. Juices from the liver and pancreas continue to break down food in the first part of the small intestines. In the second part of the small intestines, the food is absorbed into the body through the blood.

The final stage of the digestive system is the large intestine where food that the body does not need or is unable to break down is sent. It later leaves the body as waste.

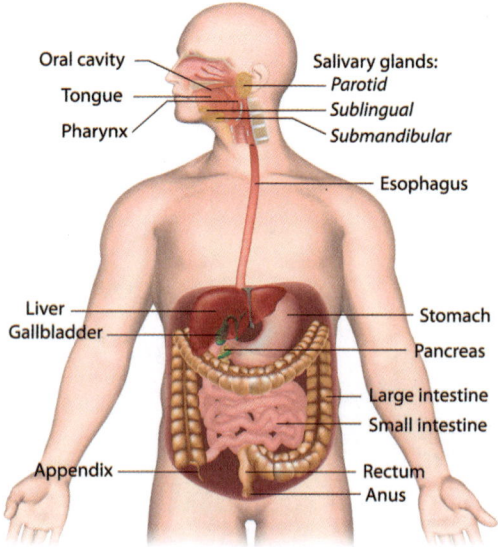

The Digestive System

184

Project 22 – The kidneys are amazing organs

2. Listen for a second time. In your notebook, make notes about the five stages whilst listening.

3. Compare your notes with a partner and consider using these prompts:

   At first, I thought …, but now I think …

   I think … was important because …

   I made a connection when …

4. When the listening is complete, discuss the text using the 3-2-1 strategy and complete the table.

3 things I know	2 things I found interesting	1 question I have

Word builder

Vocabulary box

stomach	excretion	kidneys
digestion	enzyme	intestines
digestive	appendix	oesophagus
excretory	nutrition	pancreas

1. Read the words from the vocabulary box aloud. Sort the words into the following categories:

Basic spelling patterns	Unusual spelling pattern	Class disagrees about correct pronunciation

ICT opportunity

Search engines and online dictionaries include a feature that provides a recording of the correct pronunciation of words. Listen to these recordings and create pronunciation guides for each of the words.

2. Create a drawing of the digestive system. This could be done individually, as a group or as a class art project. Use the correct scientific vocabulary to label each part of the drawing. Discuss the functions of each organ.

3. Role play how food travels through the digestive system. Assign different roles to each other. As each part of the role play is enacted, the actors should describe the process using the accurate scientific vocabulary. Take turns to play different roles so that you can get used to using and pronouncing the vocabulary.

4. Try role playing using Jamaican Creole (JC) as well as Standard Jamaican English (SJE). Discuss the differences in tone and the effect of switching from one code to another. Do you think Standard Jamaican English (SJE) is always preferred by medical staff, or are there times when it is better to use everyday terms? Think carefully about the emotional contexts that these words can be used in and what would be more suitable.

Project 22 – The kidneys are amazing organs

Let's read

1. Look at the key below. These symbols can help us think about thinking! When we read, it is important not to only read the words, but to:

   1. think about what they mean
   2. notice what is going on inside our minds when we read.

✔	I understand this well.
*	I had an idea.
+	This seems important.
?	I am confused or unsure.

   > This idea of "thinking about thinking" is called **metacognition**. Strong students strengthen their thinking using strategies like these.

2. Discuss the idea of "thinking about thinking" and whether you ever notice or recognise your own thoughts.

3. Read the text titled *The kidneys are remarkable organs* on the next page. Use the symbols to help you notice your own thoughts as you read. Either:

   1. draw some of the symbols on strips of paper and place them on the text as you read

      or

   2. draw the symbols directly onto the page or in the margins if you have a copy of the text and are allowed to do so.

4. Share your use of symbols with a partner or with a small group. Discuss why you placed the symbols where you did and use them to prompt a discussion to improve your understanding of the text. Discuss the different strategies that help clear up confusion.

187

The kidneys are remarkable organs

Our kidneys are two bean-shaped organs situated in the abdomen above the large intestines and on either side of the central spine. They perform a vital function in the digestive and excretory systems.

One good way to understand the function of the kidneys is to imagine them as filters. They are used by the body to control the levels of sugar (glucose) in the blood and to control how much water is in the body.

Renal arteries transport blood from the heart to the kidneys. Here, the blood is filtered so that waste products are removed. These waste products are then transported as urea to the bladder, where they wait to be passed from the body along with water as urine. The useful products that are in the blood, such as glucose, are then returned to the blood stream to be pumped around the body. These nutrients and sugars are required by the organs and muscles in order to function effectively.

During exercise, the kidneys' work in controlling water levels becomes very important. When we sweat, the levels of water in the body are reduced. It is important to stay hydrated before, during and after exercise, so that the kidneys can perform effectively and remove the waste products that build up in our blood.

When people have problems with their kidneys, they may need to undergo medical treatment. In extreme cases, some people have kidneys removed. It is possible for the human body to function with just one kidney, and this can be the case where transplants are offered from one healthy donor to someone in need. Sometimes, a family member donates a kidney to another, though this will be in a medical emergency after other options have been explored.

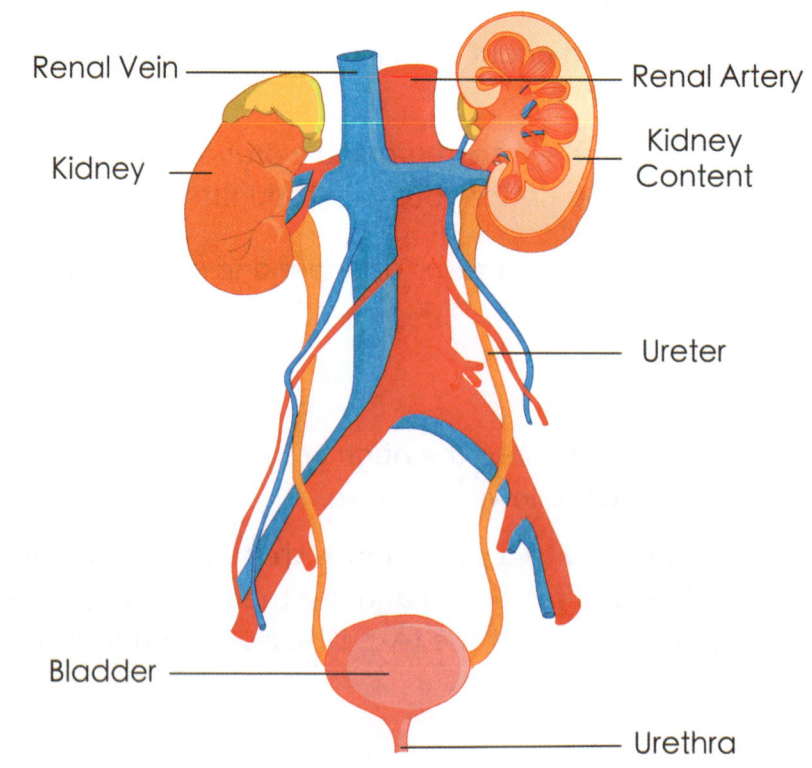

Project 22 – The kidneys are amazing organs

Grammar builder

Look and learn

An **appositive** is a noun or phrase that renames the noun it is next to. Often, this renaming gives us more information so that the text is easier to understand. Look at these examples of appositives. The noun is red and the appositive is blue.

The surgeon, an expert in kidney-transplant procedures, showed us where the operations take place.

The skeleton, a scary plastic toy used in our Science lessons, is named Harry.

1. Compare these two versions. What has been added to version 2? What is the effect of each addition?

Version 1	Version 2
Bile is stored in the gall bladder.	Bile, a vital substance for digesting fats, is stored in the gall bladder.
The small intestine is five metres long.	The small intestine, the organ where most food is absorbed, is five metres long.
A small, finger-shaped part of the digestive system is called the *appendix*.	A small, finger-shaped part of the digestive system is called the *appendix*, a part of the immune system.

2. With your partner, look at the sentences in Activity 1. Discuss how the appositive phrases help improve understanding when a novice reads each sentence.

3. Discuss the punctuation required to insert an appositive phrase into the sentences above. Can you see the commas that are used to show where the sentences join? Why do you think one sentence only requires one comma and the other two sentences require two?

4. Write a short paragraph describing a part of the digestive system. Look back at your role play in the "Word builder" lesson or your diagrams to help you. Include an appositive phrase to support the understanding of the following nouns: oesophagus, stomach, intestine, kidney and rectum.

Let's write

Work in groups for this writing project. Use texts, research, prior knowledge and discussions to find the information you need. Then decide how you will prepare your project to present to the class.

1   Complete the sentences.

   1   We have decided to create a project about the _____ system.

   2   We will research this by _____.

   3   The reason we think this is an important system is _____.

2   Your presentation will need to include the following elements:

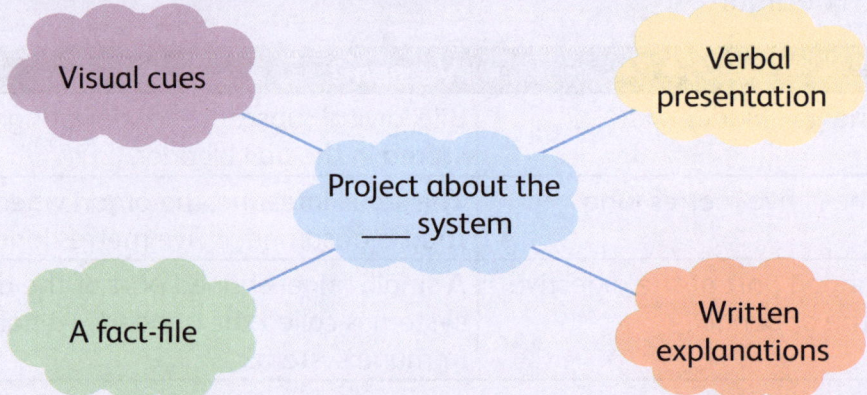

Plan the tasks required for your project and how to make sure that they are all completed in the time specified by your teacher.

3   Create your presentation. Everyone should be involved in writing and researching. Use the "Editor's checklist" to ensure that the explanations are clear and to help the audience understand.

Editor's checklist

- accurate technical vocabulary
- appositive phrases
- signal words for the flow of ideas
- organised paragraphs

Project 23

Speaking and listening

Listen to each other tell stories of visits to the doctor or to the hospital. This should be an informal discussion, sharing and asking each other questions. Remember to follow the communication protocol, but most importantly, you should feel comfortable speaking. If you do not want to answer a question or go into detail, that is fine. You need to respect one another's decisions.

1. Work in small groups. Take turns to share experiences of when you visited a nurse, doctor or hospital. Do you go regularly? Does anyone in your family require medical treatment or medicines regularly to treat a condition?

2. Listen to a news report or a story of a medical situation. With the approval of your teacher, watch a Jamaican news channel on YouTube and discuss the language used. Compile questions to find out more information.

   For example: https://www.youtube.com/watch?v=EBhum5CELBU&ab_channel=TelevisionJamaica

3. Use the KWI prompt to support your listening and reflection on the story.

K	W	I
What I **KNOW**.	What I **WANT** to know.	Something I thought was **INTERESTING**.

Word builder

Look at these words. Note that *chr* is pronounced as *kr*.

| chronic | chronically | chromosome | chromosomal |

1. Use a dictionary or online tool to search for other words that begin with *chr-*. Is *chr-* always pronounced the same way?

ICT opportunity

Carry out an internet search to find words that contain *chr*. It is very difficult to use a book for this kind of search, but computers can perform this function very well.

- Remember, you must be sensible when you are online. Refer to the "Speaking and Listening" lesson in Project 1 for online safety rules.

2. Use each of the words from the word list in a sentence. Find the definition of each word first, then try to use it in a medical context.

3. Look at these words. In which words is *ch* pronounced as *k*? Use an online pronunciation application to check your answers.

| ache   lunch   monochrome   chariot   inches
characterisation   holepunch   catch |

Project 23 – When we need medical help

Let's read

Read the letter and complete the following tasks.

> 15 Hummingbird Road,
> Montego Bay
>
> 15 March 2023
>
> Dear Sirs,
>
> This letter is written from urgent necessity. We are grateful for the time you will take to consider the information carefully. May we take this opportunity to request that the information be kept in the strictest confidence. For this reason, at this stage in our enquiries, the individual concerned will remain anonymous.
>
> As you will be aware, medical science has advanced rapidly in recent years. Modern medicine, it seems, can achieve near miracles. One recent advance has given us hope where before there was none.
>
> A student at the school has been diagnosed with a chromosomal disease, which has caused the deterioration of his kidney function. As well as causing significant and chronic pain, the disease has limited the time he has to attend school. Consequently, his chances of a good education have been damaged.
>
> His family now are required to provide him with constant medical care, including weekly trips to the hospital. Despite reports of an unlikely recovery, news has reached us of a new treatment that may be able to repair some of the damage to his kidneys. However, the treatment will cost many thousands of dollars, and his family are not in a position to afford the medical bills.
>
> As such, we write to ask for assistance. We hope that you will understand the need for this treatment and consider this a worthy cause. If you would be willing to go some way to supporting this family, through offering financial assistance towards this new therapy, please contact us on the address given at the head of this letter.
>
> Yours faithfully,
>
> *Glenmore Higgins*

1. Use the RAFT strategy to develop an understanding of the text:

   Role – What is the role of the author of this letter?

   Audience – Who is the intended audience? How can you tell?

   Format – What are the features of the way that this letter is presented?

   Theme – How would you summarise the main content of this letter?

2. Use the reasoning response symbols to develop an awareness of your own understanding of this letter.

✔	I understand this well.
*	I had an idea.
+	This seems important.
?	I am confused or unsure.

3. Choose three sentences that seem the most difficult to understand. Discuss as a class and share strategies for decoding the meaning.

4. Find and copy three factual sentences and three sentences which rely on opinion or emotions. Explain the purpose of these emotional techniques, in the context of this letter.

5. Think carefully before answering these questions. They require inference.

   1. Why do the authors not give the patient's name?
   2. How much do we know about the new treatment?
   3. Have the family asked for the money themselves?

Extra challenge

Many charities and causes ask for money from individuals and from businesses. Very often these causes are legitimate. However, some requests are fraudulent.

Look up the meanings of the words *legitimate* and *fraudulent*.

Discuss strategies you can use for deciding whether a request is legitimate or whether it is fraudulent.

Project 23 – When we need medical help

Grammar builder

1. Look at the letter in the "Let's read" lesson. Can you identify the tenses in the letter? Look for examples of past, present and future tenses.

> **Look and learn**
>
> Use: The **continuous tense** is used to describe an action that is ongoing or that is not complete.
>
> Form: The continuous tense is formed by using the verb *to be* with an *-ing* verb.
>
> I am writing to ask for help.
>
> We were hoping that you will help.
>
> You are reading about a very important issue.
>
> Use: The **perfect tense** is used to describe a verb that is a completed action. It may also be used with events that occurred at an unspecified time in the past.
>
> Form: The perfect tense is formed by using a form of the verb *to have* as an auxiliary.
>
> I had written to ask for help.
>
> We had hoped that you would be able to help.
>
> You have read about a very important issue.

2. How many examples of the continuous tense and the perfect tense can you find in the letter in the "Let's read" lesson?

3. Choose three sentences to adapt and rewrite using the perfect form of the verbs.

4. Formal language and formal letters require very clear sentences and paragraphs. The order of ideas and progression of argument has to be signalled very precisely. Look for signal words or phrases that are used to guide the reader through the structure of the reasoning in the letter.

Let's write

1. Plan and write a formal letter to a business requesting funds for a cause. Possible causes could include funds for:

   - medical treatment
   - improved facilities within a medical centre
   - improving the school facilities and resources with an impact on the health and well-being on some or all of the students
   - a local community project that will benefit the well-being or health of the community.

2. With your partner, discuss and make a list of signal words and phrases, such as *consequently* or *as a result*, which can be used to organise the thinking in a formal letter.

3. Plan your letter. Use the paragraph organiser to help you.

Paragraph	Purpose of the paragraph	Opening sentence
Introduction	Explain the purpose of the letter.	
Paragraph 1	Describe the background information.	
Paragraph 2	Explain in more detail.	
Paragraph 3	Describe the action required.	
Concluding	Reminder of the importance of the cause.	

4. Write your first draft. Make sure that you include:

   - signal words
   - formal style
   - technical vocabulary appropriate to the task.

5. Present your second draft of the letter in the format of a professional letter. You should make sure that it is clear and looks formal. For example, be concise, state the purpose of your formal letter in the introduction, keep to the topic, use an appropriate tone and use an appropriate format and style of presentation.

Project 24

Speaking and listening

1 Share ideas with the class.

   1 What do you understand by the word *puberty*?

   2 Talking about puberty can make some people feel embarrassed. Why do you think some people get embarrassed?

   3 What kind of language techniques can we use to support these discussions?

2 1 Picture your life and make brief notes about your predictions:
   - 1 year from now
   - 5 years from now
   - 20 years from now
   - 50 years from now.

   2 In pairs, discuss what your hopes, fears and questions are for the future.

3 Listen to your teacher read the poem *Springtime of life*. Close your eyes when you listen and then discuss and answer the following questions in pairs.

1. Who is the poem about? Why do you think this?
2. What do you think the first and second lines mean?
3. Why is the person being *rearranged*?
4. What is meant by "as my body breaks free"?
5. What does "But for now" mean?
6. What does the title imply?

Springtime of Life

Puberty is working against me,
Puberty wants to bring me down,
My voice has broken, it's left me unspoken,
what makes me has changed, I'm being rearranged
from duckling to swan, I'll soon be reborn.

They say, "Wait and see … you will love the new you!"
I want to agree as my body breaks free.
But for now, I am shy and often feel blue.
What are all these feelings I cannot deny?

by Heather Raymond

4 As a class, discuss your answers and exchange your ideas. If you had to choose an alternative title, what would it be?

Project 24 – Understanding puberty

Word builder

Vocabulary box

produce	reproduction	producing	development
reproduce	produced	reproducing	developing
production	reproduced	develop	developed

1. Read the words from the vocabulary box in a call-and-response form. Listen carefully to the syllable pattern and the rhythm of each word. How does adding a prefix alter the pronunciation?

2. Identify the two root words. Identify all the suffixes in the vocabulary box. Write down three other words that end with each suffix. Try to identify how each suffix alters the meaning or use of the word.

3. Research an appropriate scientific text about puberty or becoming a teenager. Find all the technical words and make a list of them. Then complete a table like the one below.

Word	Meaning	Example in a sentence	Spelling strategies	Everyday synonyms/ slang terms

Extra challenge

Find all the technical words and develop a way to test:
- pronunciation
- spelling
- understanding of meanings.

You could divide into groups to develop different ways to test each other, and then share these techniques with the rest of the class.

Let's read

The extract below is from the poem *Seven Ages of Man* and is part of the comedy *As You Like It* written by William Shakespeare in the 16th century. It is a speech of a philosopher, Jaques, talking to Duke Senior. Jaques is a man who likes to sound clever, but he is described as melancholy and a pessimist or a cynic. He talks about the *seven ages*, which is his way of describing the different stages of a person's life.

1 Think about the following questions as you read the text.

1. What are the seven ages of man described? Can you summarise them in one word each?
2. What challenges does each age bring?

Seven Ages of Man

All the world's a stage,
And all the men and women merely players;
They have their exits and their entrances,
And one man in his time plays many parts,
His acts being seven ages. At first, the infant,
Mewling and puking in the nurse's arms.
Then the whining schoolboy, with his satchel
And shining morning face, creeping like snail
Unwillingly to school. And then the lover,
Sighing like furnace, with a woeful ballad
Made to his mistress' eyebrow. Then a soldier,
Full of strange oaths and bearded like the pard,
Jealous in honor, sudden and quick in quarrel,
Seeking the bubble reputation
Even in the cannon's mouth. And then the justice,
In fair round belly with good capon lined,
With eyes severe and beard of formal cut,
Full of wise saws and modern instances;
And so he plays his part. The sixth age shifts
Into the lean and slippered pantaloon,
With spectacles on nose and pouch on side;
His youthful hose, well saved, a world too wide
For his shrunk shank, and his big manly voice,
Turning again toward childish treble, pipes
And whistles in his sound. Last scene of all,
That ends this strange eventful history,
Is second childishness and mere oblivion,
Sans teeth, sans eyes, sans taste, sans everything.

Project 24 – Understanding puberty

2 Read through the text as a call-and-response game with your teacher:

Student A says the first line and then calls a random name, student B.

Student B repeats the sentence of student A and adds the next line, then nominates student C.

Student C repeats the last line of student B and adds the next line, etc.

As the game progresses, students will read out two lines of the poem.

3 Match each Shakespearean word with its modern synonym.

1	mewling	a	bag
2	pantaloon	b	sad
3	woeful	c	trousers
4	satchel	d	crying

4 After reading the text, answer these questions.

1. Find and copy the name of the animal compared to a schoolboy.
2. How many stages are there said to be in a lifetime?
3. What is the meaning of *merely*?
4. Why is the schoolboy's face *shining*?
5. Who is said to have a large stomach?
6. What is the meaning of his *big manly voice turning again to childish treble*?
7. *Sans* is a French word meaning *without*. What does the last line describe?
8. What meaning is suggested by the phrase *bubble reputation*?
9. What could *this strange eventful history* most likely be referring to?

G Grammar builder

In writing, there are different ways to show people or characters speaking, as shown in the table below.

Speech bubbles	Playscript	Direct quotation	Reported speech
I like to use a speech bubble.	Character: (proudly) These are the words I say.	"Another way is to use speech marks," said the wise lady.	A wise man said that you could also use reported speech.

Look and learn

To convert quotations into reported speech, imagine you are explaining what was said, but without saying the actual words.

"As long as you are back by five o'clock," said Ma.

Ma said that I had to be back by five o'clock.

It is like a news report: you are reporting the meaning of what they said, but you do not have to use their voice or their exact words. Reported speech often begins with phrases like:

He said that …

She told me that …

1. Write a dialogue based on how the body changes during puberty. This could be a dialogue of an older brother or sister explaining to a younger child what will happen during puberty.

    Remember to include:

    1. correct use of quotation marks
    2. correct use of commas in quotations.

2. Convert the dialogue into reported speech. This could be written as if the younger child is writing a personal diary entry and is recording the meaning of what they were told, but not using direct quotations.

Project 24 – Understanding puberty

Let's write

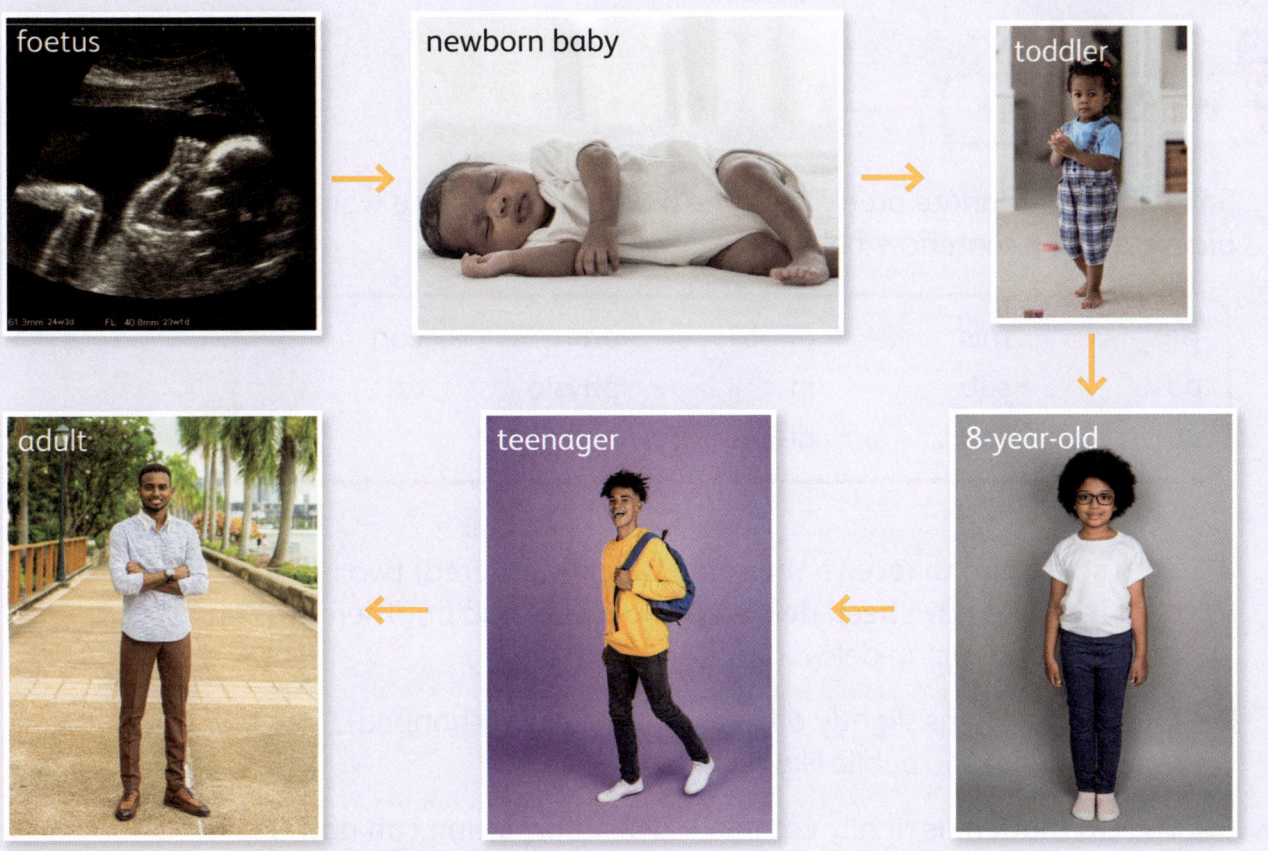

Development of a human being

As a final writing challenge for this theme, choose from the following options:

1. Write a playscript tackling some of the issues of growing up. Your language choice should show emotion. Select Jamaican Creole (JC) and Standard Jamaican English (SJE) as appropriate for each speaker.

2. Compose a poem about the hopes and fears of a child about to enter puberty. Look back at the poem *Springtime of Life* in the "Speaking and listening" lesson for ideas. Your poem should include:

   • similes
   • personification
   • rhythm.

Term 2 Unit 2 Review and assessment

Word builder

1 Select the appropriate prefix from the box to pair with the words in brackets in the sentences below.

pre	mis	photo	para	con
post	sub	in	physio	ad
un	trans	dis	re	

1 I am so excited to receive the novel which I (ordered) two months ago. It should have been delivered two weeks ago but there was an (avoidable) shipping delay.

2 This image seems slightly different; has it been (shopped)? It is not right to (lead) the public like that!

3 The (formation) is finally complete. The information can now be (leased) to everyone who was affected by the delay.

4 (Therapy) is both painful and expensive, but if I don't do it, I will be at a (advantage).

5 Shelly and Michelle (tended) to camp in their garden last Friday night, but their brother spooked them into believing there was (normal) activity during the night.

6 Yesterday, our coach told Noel that he had to (just) his attitude and improve his (par) game or he would be kicked off the team.

Review and assessment

Let's read

1. Read the letter from Sunshine to her Aunt Jen – Sunshine's mother who migrated to England. Answer the following questions.

> 25 May 1971
>
> Dear Aunt Jen,
>
> I am so used to not getting a reply to my letters that I don't even bother to wait on you anymore. I think part of the reason for that is that I don't talk to the hibiscus hedge so much these days so I write to you instead. You are not really different from the hibiscus hedge, even though you are a person, because just as how it just listens, you just sit in England and never reply. I think though that I prefer to write more than I like to talk these days, so I write to you. Sometimes I think that one day I'll get a big parcel from the post office with all my letters to you coming back unopened. I usually think that when I am trying to work out what could be keeping you from writing to me.
>
> I am very puzzled,
>
> Sunshine

1. Why do you think Sunshine continues to write to Aunt Jen even though there are no replies to her letters? How do you know this?

2. Sunshine compares Aunt Jen to the hibiscus hedge. What does that tell you about how Aunt Jen treats Sunshine?

3. How does Sunshine feel about Aunt Jen? Quote two phrases or sentences from the letter which support your view.

 **Grammar builder**

1. Reflexive pronouns are used to refer to the subject of a sentence. In the example below, *himself* is used to refer to George, who is the subject of the sentence.

   George saved for months and bought himself an expensive watch for his birthday.

   Use the following reflexive pronouns to make sentences of your own.

   | myself | yourself | himself | herself | ourselves | yourselves | itself |

 **Let's write**

Create an advertisement that could be displayed on your school's noticeboard. The advertisement should aim to persuade the student population that they will benefit from joining the newly formed *Fitness and Exercise Club*.

In addition to targeting your audience, you will need to use slogans, opinions, rhymes and alliteration. You may also use some Jamaican Creole (JC). Be careful not to offend anyone with your advertisement.

TERM 3 Unit 1

Project 25

Speaking and listening

1. Discuss food with your partner. Find a food you both like, a food you both dislike and a food that only one of you likes. Repeat this with other people in the class.

2. Jamaica is a diverse country. Discuss as a group the many similarities and differences shared by Jamaicans.

   1. Why is diversity important?
   2. What would the world be like if we were all identical?
   3. How do you react when someone disagrees with you or has different tastes or habits?

We are all Jamaicans and we are all different.

Extra challenge

Try taking on the roles and opinions of someone else. Role play someone who loves a food that you dislike, or dislikes a food that you like. Make sure you think about their feelings and do not disguise your own feelings as theirs.

Was it easy? Why or why not?

Being able to understand and appreciate other people's thoughts and feelings is called **empathy**.

Word builder

Vocabulary box

population	Caribbean	culture	diversity
experience	advantage	immigrant	cooperation
ethnic	disadvantage	Jamaican	community

1. Read the words from the vocabulary box to your partner. Sort them into the following categories:

Words I can read and understand.	Words I can read but do not fully understand.	Words I am not sure how to pronounce.

2. Use a dictionary or glossary to find the meanings of each word you do not fully understand. Create a table like this one.

Word	Meaning or meanings	Example sentence	Related words
Jamaican	A person or object that …		

3. Consider the power of a word. What about the power of the word *Jamaican*? How do you feel if someone calls you Jamaican? What would it feel like to be told you were not Jamaican? Discuss with your partner. Write down all the feelings you have about being Jamaican.

Extra challenge

Discuss this statement: Human language is one of the most powerful tools in history.
1. Do you agree?
2. How do words affect you? Do they affect your life, your feelings, your opinions, your thoughts? Do they bring you joy or misery?
3. Is it the words that have power, or the people who use them?
4. Have you ever been told to be careful how you say something? Why do you think this is?

Project 25 – A diverse country

Let's read

1 Look at the images and answer the following questions.

   1 Name a parish capital identified on the map.

   2 Name two places to the south of the country.

   3 What is the population of Portmore?

   4 Look at the three graphs. What is the name of each type of graph?

   5 How could you summarise what each image shows in one sentence?

   6 Is the information shown in each image fact or opinion? Explain how you know.

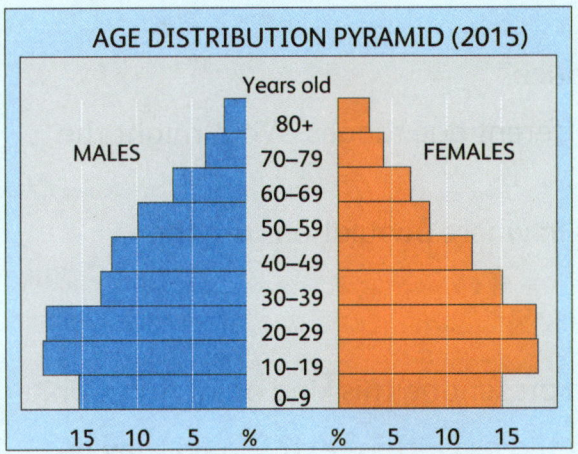

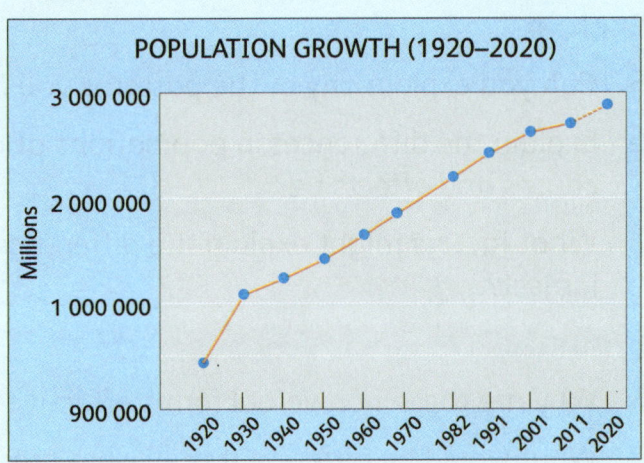

209

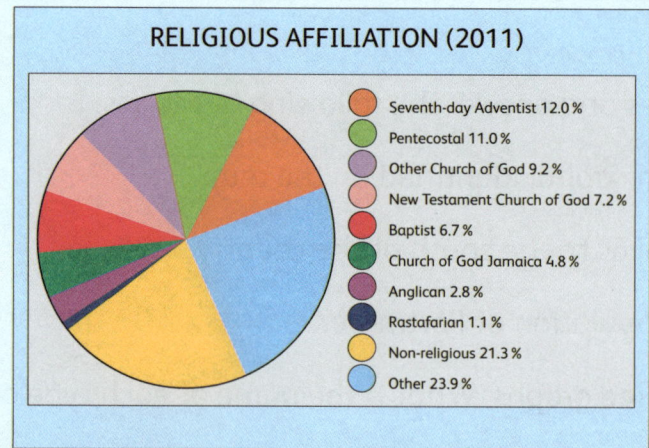

Research and study skills

Describe

The information above is shown in various forms.

1. Describe the meaning of each diagram.
2. What is the purpose of each?

Interpret and summarise

3. Interpret each diagram and give a summary of the main information or the patterns that they display.
4. Use these phrases to support your interpretations:

    1. This diagram shows that …
    2. This shows a clear pattern that …

Explain

5. Can you explain any of the patterns you notice?
6. Explain the differences in populations of different age ranges. What might the causes and effects be?
7. What factors might explain the differences in where populations are the largest?

Evaluate

8. Why are these non-verbal forms effective in presenting this kind of information?
9. What would be different if they were presented as written text? Would they be easier or harder to understand? Why?

Grammar builder

Remember ☆☆☆

We have learned how to use different tenses and aspects of verbs:
- past, present, future
- continuous, perfect.

In pairs or small groups, remind each other how to form the continuous and the perfect verb forms.

1 Correct these sentences so that the verbs and the subjects agree.

1. We goes to the park every week.
2. You forgets everything I tells you.
3. She never remember he hat or wear her smart shoes.
4. We had been sang the wrong song.
5. When I sees them, Michael and Anita always asks me for money.

Look and learn

Using the correct form of the verb with collective nouns can be tricky.

If we talk about *the class*, *the choir* or *the team*, then it seems like we are talking about lots of people, and therefore we should use a plural verb.

However, a class, or a choir is just one single group, and so we usually use the singular verb to agree with each.

2 Correct these sentences.

1. The class were really noisy.
2. In rehearsals, Amir sing beautifully but the choir sound awful.
3. The team's shirt were striped red and blue.
4. The team was wearing their away kit.
5. Although most of the class was ready, most of the boys was not listening to the instructions.

3 Challenge a partner:

1. Write three of your own sentences using the collective nouns *class*, *choir* and *team*.

2. Change the correct verbs and make them incorrect (so they do not agree with the collective noun).

3. If you are unsure of your sentences, ask your teacher to check them before you present them to your partner.

4. Ask your partner to write the correct sentences in their notebook.

Project 25 – A diverse country

Let's write

Compare the written summary with the information on the graph about the world's population growth.

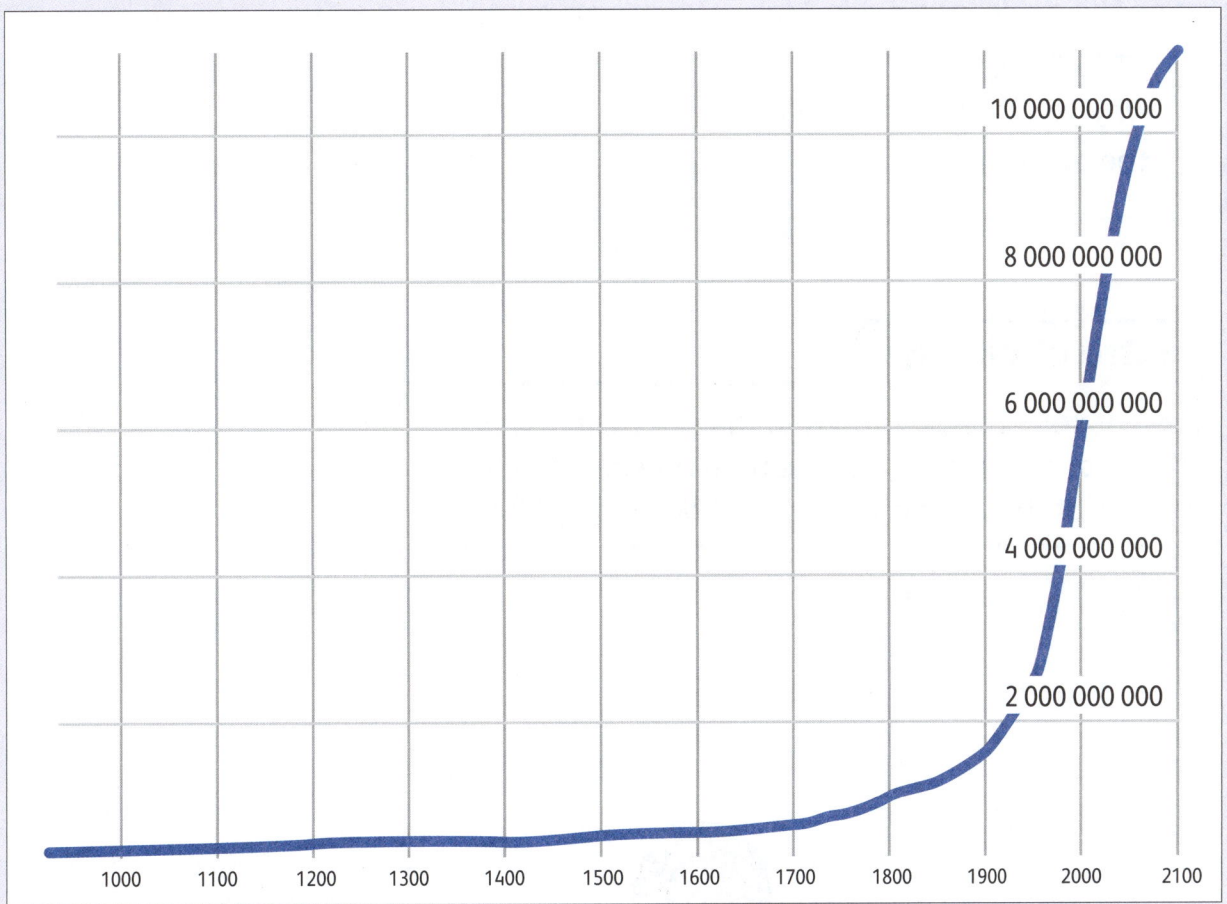

As you can see from this graph, world population grew steadily until it began to increase more steeply around the 18th century. The 20th century has seen a rapid increase, despite the many deaths in two World Wars. The initial rise can be attributed to developments in the Industrial Revolution, though it is advances in medicine and agriculture that have caused the unprecedented rise of recent years. The projections for future growth show that we expect the population to exceed 10 billion by the end of the 21st century. This poses the question of whether the Earth can sustain a human population of such proportions.

1 Evaluate the writing of this interpretation. Is it effective?
2 What language choices have been made? Are verbs, adjectives and adverbs used effectively?
3 Which phrases link the sentences and support understanding for the reader?

ICT opportunity

With your teacher's guidance, research population growth or another statistic for Jamaica. Provide a written interpretation, using the model as a guide. Make sure you explain:

- **what** is happening
- **why** you think it is happening
- **the effect** you think it will have.

Extra challenge

Present your interpretations to the class. Discuss the effectiveness of the language used and decide which aspects of the writing model could be adapted further.

Project 26

Speaking and listening

Your teacher will read aloud two texts. Whilst you listen, cover the texts.

1. Listen to different personal accounts of people who came to the Caribbean. Save questions or observations until the accounts have finished.

An indentured servant's account

Maybe I misunderstood the recruitment officer. He promised us poor villagers a better life. In exchange for transportation, boarding and an allotment of land, we were to work for four to seven years on the plantations. Somehow, I did not expect to be travelling so far from my homeland. Somehow, I did not expect the journey to be under such cramped and depressing conditions. Where is the better life I was promised?

When we arrived, we realised that we were bound by contracts with harsh penalties and we were not free. Instead, we were tied to the plantations; owned. In addition to the long working hours, we could not leave the plantations without permission. To do so was to risk imprisonment. The greedy plantation owners often schemed and added years to the contract period even when the terms were fulfilled.

A slave's account

I was frightened and did not know what horrors were waiting for me when I was captured. I was chained and shoved into the bowels of a large ship with many other captives from my country. Some I knew, others were from different tribes. There was no room to move round and we were given very little food and water to sustain us on this frightening voyage. Of course, many got sick from diseases and died in the cramped space. The heat and stench were unbearable. In our homelands we were warriors and leaders, but on the ship we were chained and treated like animals. When we got to Jamaica, we were separated, washed and oiled for auction. It was demeaning to stand on the auction block knowing that we would be owned and worked by whoever bought us.

2 Compare and contrast the experiences from the two texts.

1. Answer the questions in your notebook.
   - What are the common themes and the major differences?
   - Do any of these accounts remind you of stories you know or of the experience of someone you know?
   - What do you think about these stories and experiences?
   - How do they make you feel? Why?

2. Discuss your answers in groups. Decide on a fair way to listen to questions or observations and on a fair way to ensure that everyone gets a chance to speak.

3. In groups, discuss this saying: *Out of many, one people*.

   - What are its positive interpretations?
   - What might someone say to criticise it?
   - How does it make you feel? Why?

   Remember to follow the communication protocol, focusing on what to do when you hear something that makes you want to ask a question.

4. Come together as a class for a plenary discussion with your teacher.

Project 26 – Ancestors and descendants

Word builder

Vocabulary box

immigration	descendent	interrelationships	population
immigrant	ancestor	transportation	slavery
emigration	consequences	sustainability	enslavement

1 Read the words from the vocabulary box. Break each word into parts. Look for syllables, prefixes, suffixes and root words to chunk them together into easier units to learn, understand and remember.

2 Play a game in a circle. One person says a word out loud from the vocabulary words and spells the first three letters. Then the next person in the circle spells out the remaining letters. If you complete a spelling correctly, you get a point and choose the next word to spell. If you are wrong, the next person in the circle tries to spell the word to get the point.

3 Read the following passage. Complete the text by inserting the missing letters in the words.

> The p _ p _ l _ t _ _ n of Jamaica has increased over time. The tr _ nsp _ rt _ t_ _ n of slaves in colonial times to Jamaica was a major factor. The c _ ns _ q _ _ nc _ s of this is that there are many people who are a d _ sc _ nd _ nt of a former slave, or of someone who came to Jamaica as an _ mm _ gr _ nt. As such, the current community is diverse in its profile.

ICT opportunity

Use presentation software to create a spelling challenge for the words from this topic. You could create slides that present words with missing letters, or where the words are jumbled by syllables.

Extra challenge

Create a short paragraph using the words *immigration* and *emigration*. Make the differences in meaning clear by the context of the sentences.

217

Let's read

1 Read the letter and decide whether it is personal or formal. Find and copy phrases that show you which it is.

> 26 August 1991
>
> Trinity Village, St. Lucia
>
> Dear Georgia,
>
> Here I am. In a little house on a hill. Mrs John lives here on her own and I've got her son's old room which is separated from the parlour, that's the living room, by a curtain. It's got two big wardrobes full of old stuff and the bed creaks – can you hear it? I'm sitting on it now drinking a glass of ginger ale and talking to you. Everything's strange and different. Fancy this, me being halfway across the world and you being there. It feels odd.
>
> The village is tiny. There's one road all the way through it with brightly coloured houses on each side. At the bottom of the road, then a few steps down the main highway, there's a beach with black sand, because of the volcanoes. Black sand, imagine. I take off my shoes and sit down on the black and blue shore, and let my feet get wet. And all over this place the plants are a lush green, the leaves and flowers are swollen with it; I'll dry some orchids for you and bring them back.
>
> Most of all it's hot, I mean hot, like Sekon, maybe hotter. Everyone in the village stares at me wherever I go as if I had an orange head with squares on it. The children whisper as I walk past sweating through my vest. Mrs Monk who lives round the corner from Mrs John sits on her porch and says, "Walk so fast, something burning?" So I've slowed down but they still stare. It makes me want to go home and be around people who understand the inside of me.

2 Complete the table below with details and phrases about the senses from the text.

Sight	Sound	Taste	Smell	Touch

3 Using evidence from the text, explain whether you think the author is having a positive or a negative experience in the Caribbean. How does the text show and hide her feelings? When her feelings are hidden, what clues did you use to guess?

Project 26 – Ancestors and descendants

Grammar builder

Remember ☆☆☆

Look at these punctuation marks.

:   …   –   ( )

Can you name them? Write a sentence using each one to show that you understand how to use them.

Colon: this is used to introduce a list or an idea.

Ellipsis: this represents a pause or something left unsaid.

Dash and **brackets**: these can be used to separate information that is extra detail but not vital to the sentence.

1. Copy this passage. Find suitable places to insert a comma, an ellipsis, a dash and brackets. There may be more than one correct answer.
   - Compare with your partner and decide which punctuation you prefer.

> I had just one thought on my mind to finally pluck up the courage to make new friends. Ever since I moved here carrying my scuffed suitcase I have been too shy to talk to anyone. I guess well, I guess I am just not the confident type. There is that boy in my class the one with the nice smile. Maybe he will be my friend.

2. Look at the following table which gives the purpose and an example of punctuation. Create a new example for each punctuation mark.

Punctuation	Purpose	Example
?	Asking a rhetorical question	Can you believe it?
:	Introducing a list or an important thought	I know exactly what you'll say: I should never have gone in the first place.
( )	Inserting a small detail or comment	I received your letter yesterday (loved the funny poem – thanks!) and read it straight away.
!	Highlighting a surprising fact or emotional response	I am FUMING!

Let's write

Imagine you have come to Jamaica and you are experiencing it for the first time.

Compose an emotive letter to relatives back in the country you travelled from using the information in the chart below. Follow this writing process.

Initial choice

Choose from the following options:
1. A slave transported to Jamaica
2. An immigrant seeking a new life. This could be set in the past or in modern times.

Planning stage

Develop a paragraph plan to give some structure to your writing.

Paragraph 1 – Introduction: Greetings? Health? Safety?

Paragraph 2 – Describe the journey

Paragraph 3 – Describe arriving

Paragraph 4 – Describe settling in a little

Paragraph 5 – Conclusion and goodbyes

Details

Personal letters are full of thoughts and feelings, and the best make descriptions come alive through writing experiences that express the five senses. Make sure you conjure up the emotions and the sensory details that express the personal experience as fully as possible.

Writing

Use this writer's checklist for a personal letter:
- Correct letter format
- Informal language choice
- Punctuation appropriate and accurate
- Thoughts and feelings described
- Sensory details described
- Rhetorical questions and directly addressing the reader.

ICT opportunity

Once you have written your first draft, your teacher may ask you to redraft it on a word processing application. This will allow you to make further checks and alterations as you write. Once complete, with your teacher's permission, these could be posted as part of a class blog.

Project 27

Speaking and listening

1. Your teacher will read a poem aloud about Christopher Columbus and his first voyage. Do not worry if you do not understand everything. Listen to the words and phrases and try to imagine the journey.

The Pull of Birds

Colón, son and grand-son of weavers
rejected that calling but did not
neglect craft (keeping two sets of books).
On his first voyage, landfall receding
(where was Japan?) he sailed on

praying for a miracle to centre him
in that unmarked immensity, as warp to woof.
And suddenly from the north a density
of birds flying south, their autumn migration
intersecting his westward passage.

At such an auspicious conjunction, his charts
he threw out, the flocks drew him south
across the blue fabric of the Atlantic.
Weary mariners buoyed by the miracle
of land soon, of birds flying across the moon.

Birds seeking to outdistance three raptors skimming
the surface of the sea and sending skyward
their doomsday utterance of hawks' bells
tinkling endlessly. Birds speeding
to make landfall at Guanahaní.

by Olive Senior

ICT opportunity

There is a recording of the poet reading her poem on *The Poetry Archive* (https://poetryarchive.org/poem/pull-birds/). Your teacher may ask you to perform a safe internet search to locate recordings of this or other similar poems. Your class could post the link on a class blog or the school website and use this to share your learning with family and friends.

- Remember, you must be sensible when you are online. Refer to the "Speaking and listening" lesson in Project 1 for online safety rules.

2. In small groups, take turns to read out the poem to each other or as a group, listen to the recording online. Discuss any words or phrases you are unfamiliar with. If you do not understand certain phrases, ask your teacher to explain its possible meaning or purpose. Talk about how the sounds of the word or phrases make you feel. What words did you notice most? Do you think the poet made certain words or sounds seem more important on purpose? Why or why not?

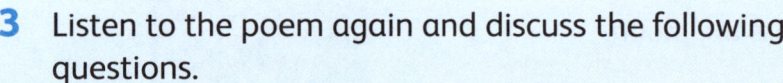

When I listen to or read a poem, I need to hear it many times before I can start to understand it in depth. Often, the first few times I hear it, I just get lost in the sounds of the words.

3. Listen to the poem again and discuss the following questions.

   1. How do you relate to this poem personally?

   2. What memories or ideas does it bring to mind? What do you imagine as you listen?

   3. Does it prompt you to think about any other stories, poems, movies or documentaries that you have seen or heard?

4. What qualities of a poem does this have? Can you find metaphors or similes? What about rhyme, rhythm or onomatopoeia?

5. Discuss as a group what makes a piece of writing poetic and how successful you judge this poem to be? If something rhymes, is that a good poem? What are the most important qualities for a poem?

Project 27 – Reflecting on colonisation

Word builder

Vocabulary box

clatter	crinkle	zap	buzz	crack
whiz	rip	gargle	burp	trickle
grumble	clink	hum	slap	

Look and learn

Onomatopoeia is the definition for a word which has a sound connected to its meaning. For example, if you hear the word *splash*, you can hear echoes of the water splashing. Some onomatopoeias can be more subtle. For example, the sound of the word *tumble* could evoke the sound and feeling of falling on a wooden floor.

1 Use an online dictionary to listen to the pronunciation of the words in the vocabulary box and to find examples of how the words are used in a sentence.

2 Write your own sentences using the onomatopoeic words from the vocabulary box. Use a variety of tenses (past simple, past continuous, present simple, present continuous) in your sentences.

3 Read each sentence and circle the onomatopoeic word. Also explain what makes the noise. The first one is done for you.

   1 The waiter slipped and the plates (clattered) to the floor. What made the noise? (the plates)

   2 After Anna brushed her teeth she gargled with mouthwash. What made the noise?

   3 Lloyd and Michael are role playing *Aliens from Mars*. Lloyd is zapping Michael with his laser gun. What is making the noise?

   4 As Lilly ran away, the bee still whizzed around by her ear. What made the noise?

   5 It was nearly lunchtime and Bob's stomach was grumbling loudly. What was making the noise?

223

Let's read

1 Read this extract from a poem titled *Colonisation in Reverse* by Louise Bennett.

Colonisation in Reverse

Wat a joyful news, miss Mattie,
I feel like me heart gwine burs
Jamaica people colonizin
Englan in Reverse

By de hundred, by de tousan
From country and from town,
By de ship-load, by de plane load
Jamaica is Englan boun.

Dem a pour out a Jamaica,
Everybody future plan
Is fe get a big-time job
An settle in de mother lan.

What an islan! What a people!
Man an woman, old an young
Jus a pack dem bag an baggage
An turn history upside dung!

Some people doan like travel,
But fe show dem loyalty
Dem all a open up cheap-fare-
To-England agency.

An week by week dem shippin off
Dem countryman like fire,
Fe immigrate an populate
De seat a de Empire.

by Louise Bennett

2 Think carefully about the following questions.

  1. Why did the author choose to write this in Jamaican Creole (JC)?

  2. The poet has used humour to make a serious point. Can you explain the main point and give evidence of the humour in the poem?

3 With your partner, role play the character from the poem as though they are a real person saying the words. What can you tell about them from what they say? Does this affect how much you agree with or enjoy the point of the poem?

> **Remember** ☆☆☆
>
> **Homonyms** are words that have different meanings but are spelled and pronounced the same. For example: *book* can mean something you read or to make a reservation.
>
> **Homophones** are words that sound the same as another word but have a different meaning and often a different spelling. For example: *to, too* and *two*.

4 Create your own verse to add to this poem. Try to match the tone, the rhythm and the rhyme scheme. Challenge yourself to include a homonym and a homophone.

Research and study skills

1. Research the historical context of *Colonisation in Reverse*. You may have to research this on the internet. Think about:

   1. What period of history does this cover?

   2. What details of the poet's biography relate to her purpose in this poem?

   3. What other works did she create? Did they have a similar purpose?

2. Create a list of sources used when researching the questions in Activity 1.

Look and learn

When you carry out research it is important that your reader knows where the information you used came from.

You need to write a reference every time you use someone else's work. This is called **citing**. You must give the source, that is the author or company that created the information, credit for their work if you wish to use it.

If you use someone else's words as your own, this is called **plagiarism**.

There are different ways of referencing sources. Your teacher or school may follow a particular style that you must follow. However, if you always keep your own reference list as you study, you can always adapt the format that is required by others.

Here is an example of an internet source you could use for your own reference list for the poem *Colonisation in Reverse*:

Louise Bennett Coverley. Poem *Colonisation in Reverse* from Jamaica Labrish, published by Sangsters (1966).
https://www.poetrybyheart.org.uk/poems/colonization-in-reverse-2/

Grammar builder

Remember ☆☆☆

Reflexive pronouns are used to refer to the subject of a verb. Examples of reflexive pronouns are: *myself, ourselves, himself, herself, themselves, yourself, yourselves.*

Look and learn

Reflexive pronouns are often misused. Look at the following sentences:
- *She gave the present to myself.*
- *She took a cake for herself.*

Only one of these uses a reflexive pronoun correctly.

Try pointing at the subject and objects of the sentence as you read. If any of them are the same, then use *-self*.

The subject is *she* so *herself* is correct, but the first sentence should read, *She gave the present to me*.

1. Choose the correct reflexive pronouns to correct these sentences about the slave trade.

   1. The slaves were left to look after myself.
   2. As they boarded the slave ships, the slave masters thought of himself as gods.
   3. If you had been in that situation, you would have sorely pitied themselves.

2. Research some of the history of the triangular slave trade between Europe, Africa and the Caribbean in preparation for writing a paragraph. Use a graphic organiser to organise your information.

3. Write a short paragraph describing the trade system. Use at least three different reflexive pronouns in your paragraph. Once you have finished, swap your paragraph with a partner and check for the correct use of reflexive pronouns.

Extra challenge

When writing historical accounts, sometimes it is appropriate to use past tenses and sometimes present tenses. Look through each other's writing about the slave trade and identify the tenses being used. Could the writing be improved by switching to a different tense? Why? Why not?

Let's write

1. Read the poem on the theme of slavery. Discuss it with a partner or in groups, focusing especially on the word choice made by the author.

Passing the Grace Vessels of Calabash

Our foreparents carved on
(lest they forget) maps, totems,
symbols and secret names,

creating art when some
would claim we existed
in beast state.

Every negro in slavery days
had their own
hand-engraved calabash.

So they'd drink water from
grace vessels, their lips
kissing lines of maps

leading back to Africa,
to villages where relatives
waited for years

before they destroyed
the cooking pots
of the ones who crossed.

by Lorna Goodison

2. Compose your own poem on the theme of slavery or colonisation. Use one of the poems you have read as a model. You might choose to change the verse length or the patterns of rhymes for your own poem. Include the elements of poetry which are listed in the "Editor's checklist".

Editor's checklist

Make sure you are using poetic techniques like:

- senses
- similes and metaphors
- onomatopoeia
- verses.

Project 28

Speaking and listening

1. Prepare a set of interview questions to ask the people shown in the image. The aim of the interview questions is to find out:

   1. their sense of being Jamaican
   2. an understanding of their heritage
   3. their experience of Jamaican culture
   4. their ambitions and the challenges they face.

2. Take on the role of one of the people from the images. You will be interviewed using the questions prepared by another student. Your aim is to respond to the questions in a way that demonstrates an understanding of the thoughts and feelings of the man or woman you are role playing.

   Spend a few moments jotting down ideas on how you would answer questions on the topics in Activity 1.

3. Take it in turns to be in the hot seat – the interview chair. First, this could be done in pairs as a practice, then performed as if on an interview show for TV. The aim is for the interviews to show:

   1. knowledge of the different experiences of people living in Jamaica
   2. empathy for the thoughts and feelings of the diversity of people living in Jamaica
   3. an understanding of how different individuals may perceive their community.

ICT opportunity

Use recording equipment to make a video or audio recording of the interviews. These can then be played back and used to support the written task.

Word builder

Vocabulary box

diaspora   miscellaneous   diversification   variance

1. Read the words from the vocabulary box. Do you recognise any of them? Can you infer the meaning by looking for root words hidden inside them?

2. Try pronouncing each of them. Is there more than one way of pronouncing each word?

3. Break them into syllables in different ways. With a partner, discuss which pronunciation seems to suit the patterns of spellings and pronunciations that you already recognise.

ICT opportunity

Use an online dictionary to play a recording of the correct pronunciation for a new word. This is a very helpful feature of internet research.

4. Make a list of unfamiliar words from your research about the different ethnic groups in Jamaica. Add these words to your journal. Use the context of their use to predict the meaning of each word, then check them using a dictionary.

Extra challenge

Organise vocabulary word lists and create a class display. Create a treasure hunt of the new vocabulary. Hide the words in different locations and challenge your classmates to find words with a specific meaning.

5. Research synonyms for the following words: *community, heritage, descendent, belief, support*.

Keep a record of these in your journal as they will be useful when you complete your work on this topic.

Let's read

The following is an extract from the *Jamaica National Heritage Trust* website.

Read the introduction and then perform your own research to find out more about the different ethnic groups who make up our Jamaican heritage.

Dis 'N Dat

Did you know?

This section contains a motley group of Jamaican heritage trivia – items that we think are important but fall into no particular category. We hope you will enjoy browsing them.

The people who came

Our rich Jamaican heritage is depicted by our motto "Out of Many One People". Although over 90 % of our population is comprised of individuals of African descent, the contribution of other ethnic groups such as the Indians, the Chinese, the Germans, the Jews and the Syrians/Lebanese to the social and economic development of the country cannot go unnoticed.

Africans

The first Africans arrived in Jamaica in 1513 as servants to the Spanish settlers. These Africans were freed by the Spanish when the English captured the island in 1655. They immediately fled to the mountains where they fought to retain their freedom and became the first Maroons.

Source: http://www.jnht.com/disndat_people.php

1 Read the extract and then answer these questions.

1. Explain the word choice for the title of the extract.

2. What does the word *motley* mean in the first paragraph?

3. Consider the many different groups mentioned in the introduction. Are you connected to any of these groups through family, friends or your local community?

4. Read the word *comprised* in the context of its sentence. Can you infer its meaning from its use here?

2. Either through research on the website or through other readings, make your own enquiries into the history of the ethnic groups that make up Jamaica's rich cultural heritage.

Think about:
- where people have come from
- why they came
- how long they have been here
- what new things they brought with them to Jamaica.

Remember

Remember to keep your own reference list when you carry out any research.

What's your view?

Why is it positive to have diversity in a country?

Project 28 – Ethnic groups

Grammar builder

Remember ☆☆☆

Contractions are used in common words, where a letter or syllable is left out. When a word is contracted, an apostrophe is written in its place. The apostrophe causes confusion because it has two different functions:

- It represents the missing part of a word in a contraction – an **apostrophe of omission**.
- It is used to show ownership – an **apostrophe of possession**.

Write a sentence with an example of an apostrophe of possession and an example of an apostrophe of omission.

1. Play the *Contraction Reaction* game. This will improve your use of contractions and is a good opportunity to think about the different ethnic groups in Jamaica.

   1. In a circle, one person starts by saying, *I'm Jamaican, and I'm …*, completing the sentence with a fact about themselves. This passes around the circle, until everyone has had a chance to say a sentence. Each sentence must begin with the contraction, *I'm …* .

   2. Now, play the game by role playing a particular ethnic group. For example, you could say: *I'm Indian and my forefathers brought betel leaves and jackfruit to Jamaica.*

2. Contractions may cause some false homophone mistakes.

   1. Discuss the following homophones:
      - they're, there, their
      - we're, where, were, wear
      - it's, its
      - you're, your

   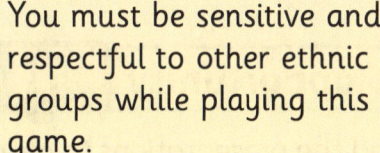

   You must be sensitive and respectful to other ethnic groups while playing this game.

   2. Create a short presentation demonstrating the correct use of each homophone and a way to remember when to write which word.

Let's write

In a small group, choose one ethnic group that you have studied or learned about. Your task will be to create a presentation about the practices, heritage, experiences and contribution of that group to the culture of Jamaica as a whole.

Use the following writing process to create a strong presentation.

Collect notes
Discuss your readings and the responses from the questionnaires. Collect notes on the facts and figures you already know and then decide which areas you need to research further.

Visual representations
Decide on what diagrams, maps, charts, graphs or tables will support your presentation and create them as part of your research.

Writing
Use the following checklist to ensure your presentations are effective:
- Use signal words or phrases: *One of the most important factors is …*
- Refer to the audience directly: *As you will see from this chart …*
- Use factual, precise language: *The first Chinese immigrants arrived by ship in …*

When all presentations are prepared, share them with the class. After each presentation, ensure there is time for a Q&A feedback session. Follow the class's communication protocol during the feedback session.

ICT opportunity
Upload the presentations to a class blog under the title *Did you know?* This could be an excellent way of sharing your learning with other schools.

Project 29 – The Caribbean

Project 29

Speaking and listening

1. Look carefully at the map with a partner. Then answer the questions.
   1. How many of the countries can you name?
   2. Have you ever visited another part of the Caribbean?
   3. Do you have friends or family who live in another part of the Caribbean?

2. What unites the Caribbean? Discuss with the class the shared experiences of the Caribbean people. What is the same across the Caribbean? What is different? How important are the differences and similarities?

3. Listen to a song or a poem about people in the Caribbean. Can you think of any movies, documentaries or books about this theme? What can you remember about them?

Extra challenge

Create a short verbal presentation for a visitor to Jamaica explaining the relationship that Jamaica has with the rest of the Caribbean. This could be created as part of a tourist guide.

Word builder

1. Use a dictionary, an encyclopedia, reading texts or an internet search with the supervision of your teacher to create a Caribbean alphabet. Some of the entries have already been filled in.

A	Antigua ambarella	B	Basseterre	C	cocobey	D		E	
F		G		H		I		J	
K		L		M		N		O	
P		Q		R		S		T	
U		V		W		X		Y	
Z									

2. Try to collect one or two more words for each letter, for example:
   - proper nouns
   - common nouns
   - adjectives.

3. Share your Caribbean alphabet with the class. Are there any words that your classmates do not know?

4. In groups, agree on spelling and pronunciation strategies for the unfamiliar words. Do you notice that proper nouns are more likely to have different spelling patterns? Can you think why this might be?

Extra challenge

Play this drama game. Sit in a circle. The first person says a sentence using as many words as they can beginning with *A*, for example: *I ate an ambarella with Anita from Antigua.* Continue around the circle until you reach the letter *Z*.

Project 29 – The Caribbean

Let's read

1 Read the email and answer the following questions.

mysearch.jm

Dear Mr Allen,

I hope you do not mind, but your school's contact details were passed to me by a colleague who met you at a conference last year. Your name was mentioned when I explained that we are trying to build links with other schools in the Caribbean to set up opportunities for young students to communicate and collaborate across and among the islands. Isn't modern technology wonderful!

Please allow me to elaborate:

We have received some funds from a culture charity that should enable us to purchase some computers and to host a website which will be shared among a number of schools. As a result of this funding, we have the opportunity to create a new project that will allow students to upload blogs, written work and photographs of their projects, and to email one another.

For me, the most exciting aspect will be that students will be able to collaborate if they are from different schools, and even if they live on different islands. I see it as my personal mission to equip the young students with the skills they require for the 21st century. Who knows where technology will lead us, but I believe many people will be working in a truly international fashion.

I hope you find this an interesting prospect, and I look forward to your reply.

Best wishes,

Mr Palmer

Headteacher, Palmgrove High

1. What visual clues are there about what type of text this is?
2. How would you describe the writing style and the tone of the text? Use evidence to explain your views.
3. Summarise the main purpose of the text. Use no more than two sentences.
4. Look for the sentences containing the words *collaborate* and *elaborate*. Explain what the words mean by inferring from the sentences they are in.
5. What does the author mean by the word *fashion*?

6 Evaluate the author's argument that the project will *equip the young students with the skills they require for the 21st century*. What does the author mean by this? Do you agree that the project will provide this? What skills do you think you will need for the 21st century?

2 Use the KWL strategy to consider what information the email contains and anything of particular interest, and then focus on any further questions you would want to ask in reply. Remember that you are replying as though you are the school headteacher! Create the questions that you would respond with in order to find out specific details.

Grammar builder

1 Study the features of formal language in the table below.

Use of punctuation marks	Format of formal writing
• Commas used in the greetings of a letter or email • Colon to introduce a list or an important passage • Accurate use of commas to separate main and subordinate clauses	• Appropriate use of greetings at the beginning and end of a letter or email • Address and date for a letter • Use of bulleted lists for summarising information • Comparison of rhetorical questions and direct questions
Main and subordinate clauses	**Verb tenses and agreement**
• How to recognise a main and a subordinate clause • Lists of conjunctions and linking phrases • Recognising overuse of *and* or *then* to produce unreadable sentences	• Past, present and future tenses • Verb agreement for plural and singular • Reflexive pronouns • Perfect and continuous verb forms

2 Pick a topic from the table. Work in small groups to create a short presentation on how to use these features effectively in formal writing. Your presentation should be brief, but should also contain instructions and examples to illustrate your points.

3 Observe the presentations from the other groups. Make notes of any useful advice and of the examples they provide.

4 Write a short journal entry as a way of recording your notes. Pay particular attention to areas you think you may struggle with in your own writing.

Let's write

1. Compose a formal email to your headteacher. Choose one of the following email options:

    1. Request a class field trip to a historical site linked to the colonisation of Jamaica.
    2. Request that the school develop further links with other schools across the Caribbean.
    3. Explain how the education of Jamaicans should be tailored to the 21st century.

2. Divide yourselves into groups A, B and C to plan the email. For example, if you choose option 1 (group A), work with all the students in your class that also choose that option.

3. In your group, compose an "Editor's checklist" of what will make an effective formal email. Use no more than four bullet points and agree as a group which four should be used.

4. Plan and then write the email. Remember to include:
   - the purpose of your email
   - details of the suggestions you make
   - an explanation of the many reasons it is important
   - a final paragraph that summarises and requests a response.

> **Extra challenge**
>
> Create an attachment for your email. This could be a list of prices, a map of the suggested trip or it could be a brochure showing the benefits of using technology in modern education. Once you have created your attachment, add it to your email. Make sure you refer to it in the main email, with a sentence like: *Attached, you will find …, which shows …*

Project 30

Speaking and listening

Let's look in more detail at the shared life, history and common experience of people living in the Caribbean.

1 As part of a class discussion, share your own experiences and contact with others living in the Caribbean.

2 In groups, locate information from textbooks, magazines and journals about common historical experiences among Caribbean people. You could split up into groups and focus on a single theme for each group, such as:

- history, colonisation and slavery
- trade and economics
- politics
- sport and leisure
- entertainment: movie, music and literature.

3 1 Share your presentations with the class and be prepared to answer questions.

  2 While you are listening to other presentations, make notes so you can offer helpful feedback at the end of their presentation.

  3 Summarise your main learning points in your journal. This will help you remember and reflect on the information you have learned.

Extra challenge

Create a set of non-verbal prompts to support your information, including graphs, maps, diagrams or tables of figures. Make sure that these are used to prompt and support, rather than replace the speech of your presentation.

Word builder

Look and learn
Abbreviations are shortened versions of words or phrases.
Acronyms are a type of abbreviation in which the initial letter of a phrase is used to form a new word.

Vocabulary box

CARICOM	WHO	SCUBA
UNESCO	UN	LASER
NATO	WWF	RADAR

1. Some of the abbreviations in the vocabulary box are for international organisations and others are for inventions. Discuss which ones you have heard of and in which contexts.

2. Pronounce all the abbreviations. From your general knowledge, predict what each of them might stand for. Then use a dictionary or online search to find out the background and correct meaning of each.

3. Create a poster of the abbreviations alongside their meanings. You could use bold capitals for the main letters and smaller, fainter lowercase letters to show the complete words. Make sure you explain what the invention or organisation is, too! You might need to include a picture.

4. Technology often uses abbreviations and acronyms for new inventions. Research some abbreviations to do with computers, for example: RAM, ROM, GB, JPEG, GIF.

Project 30 – Shared experiences

Let's read

1 Read the extract and then answer the questions.

What is CARICOM?

Since 1973, The Caribbean Community Market (CARICOM) has brought together the member nations in a group that provides economic links, political unity and a voice on the world stage. The headquarters are based in Georgetown, Guyana, but there are, at present, fifteen nations and dependencies in the group. One principal aim is to support the development of less-developed countries (LDCs), through support and expertise from MDCs (More Developed Countries). The list of countries with each designation is shown in the map.

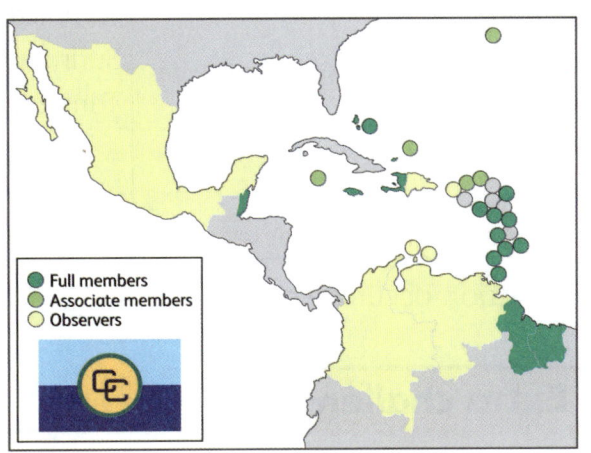

1 Explain the meanings of the abbreviations used in the text.
2 Describe the difference in meaning between *politics* and *economics*.
3 What is the meaning of the word *principal* in the context it is used?
4 Evaluate the meaning of the phrases MDC and LDC. Do you think these are useful phrases?

Research and study skills

1 Look at the list of LDCs and MDCs in the Caribbean. In groups, discuss and exchange ideas on the differences between more and less developed countries.

2 Research and then discuss in your group the differences between the LDCs and MDCs in terms of:

- Life expectancy: Does the average person in the MDCs lives longer than in the LDCs, or is there no difference?
- Education: Is the average number of years in school lower in the LDCs than in the MDCs, or is there no difference?

243

LDCs	MDCs
Antigua & Barbuda	Bahamas
Belize	Barbados
Dominica	Guyana
Grenada	Jamaica
Haiti	Suriname
Montserrat	Trinidad & Tobago
St. Kitts & Nevis	
St. Lucia	
St. Vincent & the Grenadines	

Information accurate as of 2017

Extra challenge

What is meant by the phrase *political unity*? Do you agree that this is a suitable phrase to describe CARICOM?

3 Research the background and actions of CARICOM further. Does it affect your community in any way? What is its role in justice? How is it related to other international groups such as the UN?

Grammar builder

When discussing or debating, it is important to use language that shows respect to all sides of the argument. Linking phrases can be used to express respect but also disagreement at the same time.

> **Look and learn**
>
> Here are some phrases that can be used to show respect and disagreement at the same time.
>
> - On the one hand …, but on the other hand …
> - Perhaps it is fair to say …
> - While some may agree that …, others would …
> - We strongly argue that …
> - Despite sounding like a good idea, …
> - Although people argue for …,
> - In fact, …
> - It may seem like …; however, …

1. Discuss the linking phrases from the "Look and learn" box. In pairs, write a sentence for each phrase and make sure your sentences show the balance between two different ideas if required.

2. Set up a practice debate on a topic that is not important, based on a statement such as: *Yellow is the happiest colour* or *Cats are better than dogs*. Agree to participate in a fair, respectful way, making reasoned arguments, and practise some of the linking arguments from the above task.

Extra challenge

The internet is used as a platform for many people to voice their opinions. Unfortunately, many people use it in a way that does not show respect or tolerance for other people's views. In groups, hold a short debate about the importance and power of the internet. This is a less trivial topic and will be a good opportunity for your group to use linking phrases that show respect and a balance of viewpoints.

Let's write

1. Plan a speech around this statement:

   Regional cooperation is of paramount importance.

   Discuss the meaning of the statement first, so that everyone is clear on the topic.

   Decide who will be in the for and the against groups. Then formulate a short speech outlining your opinions. Think about what you have learned so far.

2. Decide what you think a *region* is. Find out what you can about the good and bad things that can happen when regions work together and when they do things on their own.

3. Write a short speech. The language should be formal, factual and reasoned. Also take into account the audience and make sure that your arguments are clear.

   This should include some extra research to supply your arguments with evidence about:

   - economics
   - fairness and justice
   - politics and cooperation
   - community and heritage
   - diversity and international concerns

   Refer to the "Editor's checklist" to make sure your speech contains these language points.

Editor's checklist

Make sure you have used:
- linking phrases
- factual evidence
- statements of opinion
- paragraphs
- formal language.

Term 3 Unit 1 Review and assessment

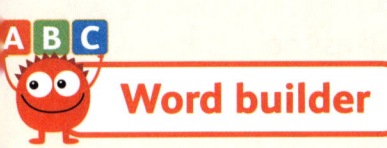

Word builder

1. Make sentences to show the different meanings of the following homonyms.

Homonym	Meanings	Example sentences
bark		
current		
spring		
address		

Let's read

1. Why might the writer have chosen to share the information below as a poem, rather than a non-fiction text?

> **As kingfishers catch fire**
> As kingfishers catch fire, dragonflies draw flame;
> As tumbled over rim in roundy wells
> Stones ring; like each tucked string tells, each hung bell's
> Bow swung finds tongue to fling out broad its name;
>
> *by Gerard Manley Hopkins*

Images:
- The kingfisher is one of the most colourful birds in England.
- Its feathers are so bright it is like they are on fire.
- Similarly, the dragonfly shines like a flame.

247

Sounds:

- The clinking sound of pebbles tossed down wells.
- The plucking of strings on a musical instrument.
- The ringing of bells as the bow swings like a pendulum and strikes the metal sides to make its sound.

2 Demonstrate your understanding of the poetic techniques below by writing five to ten lines of your own poetic verse about the beauty of something in Jamaica.

Poetic techniques:

- senses
- similes and metaphors
- onomatopoeia.

Grammar builder

One of the functions of verbs is to show tense. In the following examples, the word *work* shows when the action is taking place.

> My mother works in a lawyer's office.
> Present simple shows the frequency of occurrence of an action.

> Miss Brown is working at a bank near to my mother's office.
> Present continuous shows an action that is occurring now.

> Mr James said he had worked two years in my mother's office before moving to the bank.
> Past perfect shows an action that is completed.

1 Make sentences of your own using the tense indicated.

Verb	Tense	Sentence
ride	Present simple	
secure	Past continuous	
measure	Present perfect	
hurt	Past simple	
remove	Present continuous	
dial	Past perfect	

Review and assessment

Let's write

Write a letter to your uncle who has been studying in Australia for the last three years. Tell him about the measures being put in place to provide Jamaicans with sustainable energy sources.

- This should be a friendly or informal letter so remember to put the address in the correct position and use a more relaxed tone.

- Think about the ideas you want to include in your letter and begin by jotting them down so that you do not forget them. Plan carefully before you begin writing your paragraphs.

Develop a paragraph plan to give some structure to your writing.

- Paragraph 1 – brief introduction/greetings
- Paragraph 2 – description of the situation
- Paragraph 3 – brief conclusion and goodbye